The Mexican Revolution: A Very Short Introduction

VERY SHORT INTRODUCTIONS are for anyone wanting a stimulating and accessible way into a new subject. They are written by experts, and have been translated into more than 45 different languages.

The series began in 1995, and now covers a wide variety of topics in every discipline. The VSI library now contains over 500 volumes—a Very Short Introduction to everything from Psychology and Philosophy of Science to American History and Relativity—and continues to grow in every subject area.

Titles in the series include the following:

ACCOUNTING Christopher Nobes
ADOLESCENCE Peter K. Smith
ADVERTISING Winston Fletcher
AFRICAN AMERICAN RELIGION
    Eddie S. Glaude Jr
AFRICAN HISTORY John Parker and
    Richard Rathbone
AFRICAN RELIGIONS
    Jacob K. Olupona
AGEING Nancy A. Pachana
AGNOSTICISM Robin Le Poidevin
AGRICULTURE Paul Brassley and
    Richard Soffe
ALEXANDER THE GREAT
    Hugh Bowden
ALGEBRA Peter M. Higgins
AMERICAN HISTORY Paul S. Boyer
AMERICAN IMMIGRATION
    David A. Gerber
AMERICAN LEGAL HISTORY
    G. Edward White
AMERICAN POLITICAL
    HISTORY Donald Critchlow
AMERICAN POLITICAL PARTIES
    AND ELECTIONS L. Sandy Maisel
AMERICAN POLITICS
    Richard M. Valelly
THE AMERICAN
    PRESIDENCY Charles O. Jones
THE AMERICAN REVOLUTION
    Robert J. Allison
AMERICAN SLAVERY
    Heather Andrea Williams
THE AMERICAN WEST Stephen Aron

AMERICAN WOMEN'S HISTORY
    Susan Ware
ANAESTHESIA Aidan O'Donnell
ANARCHISM Colin Ward
ANCIENT ASSYRIA Karen Radner
ANCIENT EGYPT Ian Shaw
ANCIENT EGYPTIAN ART AND
    ARCHITECTURE Christina Riggs
ANCIENT GREECE Paul Cartledge
THE ANCIENT NEAR EAST
    Amanda H. Podany
ANCIENT PHILOSOPHY Julia Annas
ANCIENT WARFARE Harry Sidebottom
ANGELS David Albert Jones
ANGLICANISM Mark Chapman
THE ANGLO-SAXON AGE
    John Blair
ANIMAL BEHAVIOUR
    Tristram D. Wyatt
THE ANIMAL KINGDOM
    Peter Holland
ANIMAL RIGHTS David DeGrazia
THE ANTARCTIC Klaus Dodds
ANTISEMITISM Steven Beller
ANXIETY Daniel Freeman and
    Jason Freeman
THE APOCRYPHAL GOSPELS
    Paul Foster
ARCHAEOLOGY Paul Bahn
ARCHITECTURE Andrew Ballantyne
ARISTOCRACY William Doyle
ARISTOTLE Jonathan Barnes
ART HISTORY Dana Arnold
ART THEORY Cynthia Freeland

Alan Knight

# THE MEXICAN REVOLUTION

## A Very Short Introduction

OXFORD
UNIVERSITY PRESS

# OXFORD
UNIVERSITY PRESS

Great Clarendon Street, Oxford, OX2 6DP,
United Kingdom

Oxford University Press is a department of the University of Oxford.
It furthers the University's objective of excellence in research, scholarship,
and education by publishing worldwide. Oxford is a registered trade mark of
Oxford University Press in the UK and in certain other countries

First edition published in 2016

Impression: 4

Published in the United States of America by Oxford University Press
198 Madison Avenue, New York, NY 10016, United States of America

British Library Cataloguing in Publication Data
Data available

Library of Congress Control Number: 2015952190

ISBN 978-0-19-874563-1

Printed in Great Britain by
Ashford Colour Press Ltd, Gosport, Hampshire

*For Florence, Cicely, Seth, Rufus, Esmé, and Jago*

# Contents

# List of illustrations

# List of maps

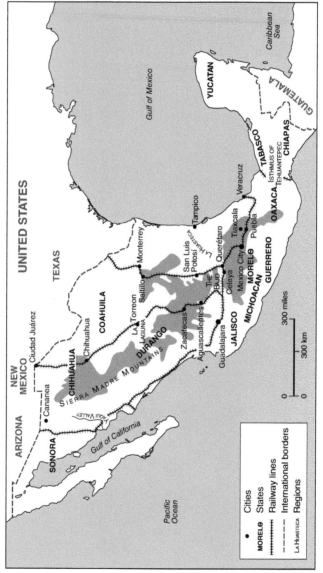

Map 1. Mexico c.1910.

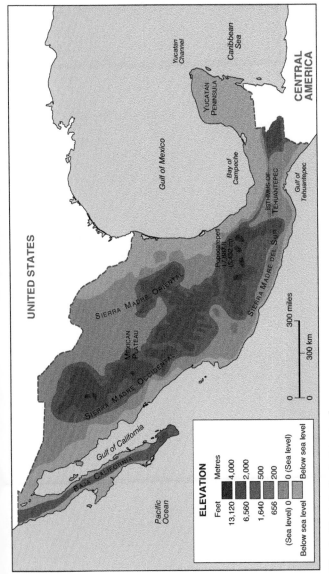

Map 2. Mexico's physical geography.

# Chapter 1
# Introduction

## Defining the Revolution

France, 1789; China, 1911; Russia, 1917: in each case, a major revolution began which decisively and lastingly affected the national history of these countries; and the Mexican Revolution of 1910 played a comparable role in determining how 20th-century Mexico would develop. Indeed, one of the chief claims of this book is that—notwithstanding some recent revisionist scholarship which tends to deflate its significance—the Mexican Revolution deserves to be included among the world's 'great' or 'social' revolutions, certainly in respect of its domestic character and impact. (Clearly, its international role was less, compared to France, China, or Russia.) It was a 'great revolution' by virtue of the scale of the fighting, the intense popular mobilization it involved, and, over time, the changes it brought about; the outcome, therefore, profoundly affected Mexico, most obviously politically, but also socially, economically, and culturally. It was not yet another Latin American barracks revolt; nor was it a mere *fiesta de balas* (a 'carnival of bullets'), a meaningless 'tale of sound and fury signifying nothing'—except, as some obtuse essentialist interpretations propose, the congenital violence and machismo of the perverse Mexican psyche.

The start of the Revolution is conventionally, and correctly, dated to 1910, since the armed insurgency which overthrew long-time president Porfirio Díaz began in that year. Of course, the causes of the insurgency, analysed in Chapter 2, were located in the past—some would say the distant colonial past. But my argument will focus on the long regime of Díaz: the 'Porfiriato', 1876–1911. The 1910 insurrection, which led to Díaz's fall a year later, began a decade of civil war, the first half of which—1910–15—witnessed mounting warfare, as guerrilla struggles and government counter-insurgency measures ('asymmetric warfare' in today's jargon) gave way to massive conventional campaigns, pitting, first, revolutionaries against the old regime (1913–14) and then revolutionaries against fellow-revolutionaries (1914–15). During these years, a liberal-democratic regime was briefly established under Francisco Madero (1911–13); and, following an army coup in early 1913, a counter-revolutionary military regime was set up under Victoriano Huerta (1913–14). Both experiments failed. Political stability and success would depend on a different strategy: one that was reformist, nationalist, scarcely liberal-democratic, but populist and inclusionary.

By 1915 the so-called Constitutionalist coalition had won; but they faced five more years of political instability, continued violence, and consequent economic dislocation. In 1920, the last successful rebellion of this decennial cycle brought to power a revolutionary faction who, through the 1920s, embarked on a successful project of pacification, state-building, and social reform. For some, therefore, 'the Revolution' ended in 1920; no subsequent armed rebellion succeeded and, by the standards of both contemporary Latin America and its own turbulent prerevolutionary history, Mexico entered a century-long period of unusual political stability, which, paradoxically though it may seem, was in good measure a product of the revolutionary upheaval of the 1910s.

As violence declined, state-building and social reform forged ahead: in the 1920s, the victorious 'Sonoran dynasty'—a clutch of revolutionary leaders from the dynamic north-western state of Sonora—laid the foundations of state power, incorporating 'mass publics' into the new politics, and confronting challenges from within (dissident generals, the Church, the foreign oil companies) and from without (a suspicious United States and, after 1929, the economic body-blow of the Great Depression). In the following decade, as 'bottom-up' pressure for social reform, released by the armed revolution, combined with the 'external shock' of the Depression, the Revolution lurched to the left, especially as President Cárdenas (1934–40) embarked on radical policies of land and labour reform, 'socialist' education, and economic nationalism (which culminated in the expropriation of the Anglo-American oil companies in 1938).

We may therefore see the Revolution, in its totality, as the work of a generation (1910–40) who first destroyed the old regime, then built a new state apparatus and, finally, carried through social reforms unprecedented in Latin America at the time. After 1940, however, the old revolutionary generation—those who had survived—shuffled off the political stage; a new leadership took power, in the context of World War II and the Cold War; and a different project—urban, industrial, conservative, and pro-American in character—replaced the radical social reformism and nationalism of the Revolution. The latter lived on, in official rhetoric, iconography, and national ritual; but, as Mexico experienced its 'economic miracle' (c.1950–80), followed by the political and economic upheavals of the 1980s and 1990s, so 'revolutionary' claims sounded increasingly hollow, if not hypocritical. The old revolutionary banner was now brandished by the political opposition—radical students, leftist opposition parties, and the 'neo-Zapatista' rebels of Chiapas, in Mexico's deep south. The Revolution remained a source of ideas, images, and inspiration, but as a programme of government—as *la revolución hecha gobierno*: the 'Revolution-made-Government'—it was a thing of the past. Thus, when it comes to understanding the character and course of the Revolution, it is the generation

1910–40 which really matters: the decade of armed violence followed by two decades of institutional reform.

## Debating the Revolution

Like any major revolution, the Mexican has been the subject of intense debate and disagreement, which show no sign of reaching closure. Recent historiographical arguments (Was it a real revolution? Was it genuinely popular? Did the revolutionary state enact the popular will or simply reward incumbent elites?) are, contrary to what some seem to think, as old as the events they seek to explain. Simplifying a complex topic, we can distinguish an old orthodoxy which depicted the armed revolution as a mass popular protest directed against a hated, oppressive, pro-foreign regime; and the ensuing *revolución hecha gobierno* as a genuine, and—at least partly—successful, attempt to satisfy popular demands by way of social and political reform. The Revolution was therefore popular, progressive, and patriotic.

This was the official position of the ruling party—after 1946 the PRI (Partido Revolucionario Institucional: Revolutionary Institutional Party)—and while, as I have suggested, that position became increasingly untenable after the 1940s, it made a good deal of sense as an interpretation of both the armed insurgency of the 1910s and, with some qualifications, the institutional Revolution of the 1920s and 1930s. (A brief further clarification: the official view stressed continuity throughout the whole generation of 1910–40; but some critics, notably Marxist historians like John Womack, saw post-1920 trends as already displaying a derogation of early revolutionary aspirations, a clear anticipation of the systemic apostasy of post-1940.)

Throughout these three decades, outspoken critics and armed rebels openly opposed the Revolution: conservatives, who hankered after the Porfirian old regime; Catholics who saw the Revolution as a vehicle of godless radicalism and freemasonry;

liberals who denounced it for sacrificing early democratic hopes on the altar of populism and authoritarianism; and radical leftists who alleged that popular aspirations had been betrayed by petty-bourgeois careerists, revolutionaries in name only.

Academic research—that is, research claiming to rise above political partisanship and making a virtue of original archival work—came thick and fast from the 1950s on, chiefly in Mexico and the US. The mainstream view still tended to align with the old orthodoxy (of a popular, progressive, patriotic revolution), but from the late 1960s new revisionist interpretations emerged and, over the next generation, they substantially transformed historical interpretations of the Revolution. In this respect, the historiography of the Mexican Revolution resembled that of other 'great' revolutions (the English and French in particular), which were also being seriously rethought. Indeed, the new interpretations and the debates which they prompted display systematic cross-national similarities: a healthy shift away from national towards local and regional perspectives; a growing critique of Marxist and class-based—some would say class-reductionist—explanations; a renewed emphasis on state-building and 'political culture'; and, by the 1990s, a broader focus on 'cultural' themes, which included questions of gender, religion, and identity.

In the Mexican context, this meant questioning—and, in some cases, denying—the popular and progressive character of the Revolution, especially the *revolución hecha gobierno* (the armed insurgency of the 1910s could not be so easily revised away). Scholars now stressed multiple and often mercenary motives and, logically, they began to question the 'black legend' of the old regime, rethinking and even rehabilitating the role of the traditional villains of story (Díaz, Huerta). They also saw the popular mobilization of the 1910s as less extensive and certainly less successful than older 'orthodox' historians had; and, above all, they depicted the revolutionary state of the 1920s and 1930s as corrupt, careerist, authoritarian, even totalitarian. The Revolution was a con trick perpetrated on a gullible, or simply unfortunate, people; the regime of the PRI was less a betrayal than a logical culmination of trends dating back at least to the 1920s if not the 1910s.

Again, these new revisionist critics belonged to different ideological camps (even if many were very respectable academic historians, who plied their trade in Mexico's rapidly expanding archives). Some, such as Enrique Krauze, stressed the betrayal of the Revolution's early liberal promises; some, among whom Jean Meyer was a commanding figure, reinterpreted Church–State conflict, inverting the old dichotomies and depicting the Catholic Church as popular, even progressive, and the revolutionary state as authoritarian and oppressive; while some, from the Left, extrapolated their critique of the contemporary PRI—an engine of political control and capitalist accumulation—back into earlier decades.

These interpretative shifts were powered, first, by trends within the discipline of history (local and regional research; a retreat from 'grand theory', especially Marxism; and cross-fertilization with other disciplines, such as anthropology and, later, 'cultural studies'); and, second, by events in the real world (globally, disillusionment with revolution as an agent of change, the decline of Communism, and the ensuing vogue for neo-liberal economic models; and, specifically in Mexico, the delegitimization of the ruling party after the 1968 repression of student protest and, even more important, the severe economic vicissitudes of the 1980s).

Whatever the causes, the current historiographical landscape—which some choose to call 'post-revisionist'—is much more complicated than that of fifty years ago. While research has become more refined and detailed, it has resulted in a fragmented picture, in which the Revolution—once the great monolith of Mexican politics and (orthodox) historiography—has been shattered into myriad shards. For some—revisionist critics of the Revolution—this is a welcome outcome: the old orthodoxy, which had underpinned the official party for decades, is thus blown to bits. (An outcome which is rather more relevant since the PRI, after twelve unprecedented years out of power, recovered the presidency in 2012.) Also, some historians, for whom 'complexity' is a major intellectual finding (rather than a statement of the stunningly obvious) and 'contingency' is a tediously recurrent mantra, this kind of historical 'splitting' is intellectually congenial. The alternative—'lumping' the data into bigger interpretations—is a thing of the past, a relic of defunct 'grand theory' which, thanks to Foucault et al., we are told, has been tipped into the dustbin of historiography.

While it might be possible to write a *Very Short Introduction* on these terms—a denial of big interpretations, an endless splitting of data, 'one damn thing after another'—it would not make much sense, nor, more importantly, would it do justice to the Revolution. For the latter, while it was—to state the stunningly obvious—'complex', did display broad trends and patterns. Some hark back to the old orthodoxy—which, just because it is old, is not necessarily all wrong—and some can be distilled, on the basis of hard historiographical labour, from recent monographs, especially those which have delved into local and regional history, adopting—rightly and productively—a 'bottom-up' approach which the old orthodoxy (obsessed with the national revolution and the new state) largely overlooked. Perhaps this is what 'post-revisionism' entails; at any rate it is the approach which this overview of the Mexican Revolution will adopt.

# Chapter 2
# The old regime and the causes of the Revolution (1876–1911)

## The historical backdrop

Some historians have suggested that the roots of the Revolution are to be found in the distant colonial period (c.1521–1821) and, certainly, many features of early 20th-century Mexico have colonial origins: a multi-ethnic population (a mixture of Indians, mestizos, creoles/whites, and a small black African population); a powerful Catholic Church; large landed estates; and many of the basic administrative divisions of the country. However, Mexico achieved independence from Spain in 1821 and the 'colonial legacy' was soon overlaid with new features; and it was these, especially those acquired during the thirty-five years of the Porfiriato (the rule of Porfirio Díaz, 1876–1911), which proved crucial in the gestation of revolution.

For fifty years following independence Mexico experienced political instability and, at best, halting economic growth. The new republic lacked the legitimacy of the old monarchy and, while liberals sought to fashion the republic in the image of the US or Western Europe, conservatives nostalgically harked back to the good old days of—supposed—colonial order and prosperity. Ideological polarization provoked a major civil war in the 1850s and, though the liberals, led by Juárez, won the war, they soon faced a renewed conservative challenge, backed by the

Catholic Church and, after 1861, by the army of France's Napoleon III. In the absence of political consensus, administrations were shaky and military interventions frequent. The state lacked adequate revenue (which is to say that Mexicans were very lightly taxed) and the politicized army took a large slice of government expenditure. Instability undermined business confidence and, compared to the major countries of South America, Mexico lacked profitable exports: the old colonial staple of silver mining had been battered by the wars of independence, while, because of Mexico's vast rugged terrain and lack of navigable rivers, transport costs were prohibitively high and foreign trade—on which the state depended for revenue—remained disappointingly low.

Mexico's geopolitical location—and proverbial untapped resources—also made it tempting to foreign predators. In the 1840s the US invaded, triumphed, and made off with half of Mexico's territory. In the 1860s French forces propped up the Emperor Maximilian, provoking a stubborn—and ultimately successful—resistance on the part of Mexico's liberals, led by Juárez. The young Porfirio Díaz, a dashing general of part-Indian origin, made his name in the campaigns against the French and, after their defeat, emerged as a serious pretender to national power. Meanwhile, the conservatives were discredited by their alliance with the invaders and the liberal party, patriotic and victorious, acquired a near-monopoly of national political power.

Thus, it was not until the late 1860s, with the invaders expelled and the Republic restored, that a semblance of stability emerged; and on this basis the economy now began a belated surge of growth. After Juárez's death in 1872, the liberal leaders jockeyed for power and, four years later, Díaz mounted a successful military rebellion. What seemed like yet another episode in the long cycle of coups and civil wars proved a major turning point—in part thanks to Díaz's political acumen (and ruthlessness), but even more because of the favourable politico-economic conjuncture that he encountered. The Mexican people were war-weary, disposed to tolerate a regime which, while not lacking popular roots, stressed the need for political stability over contestation, and economic growth over civil rights. Mexican elites, notably the so-called Científicos—a narrow coterie of businessmen-cum-technocrats who surrounded Díaz, advocated strong government and business-friendly policies; in the positivism of Auguste Comte they found a congenial philosophy which gave 'scientific' validation to their views (hence their name which, eventually, became a term of vilification).

Many defeated conservatives sympathized with this positivistic mutation of liberalism and made discreet political comebacks, which Díaz, eager to promote peace, pragmatically encouraged; just as he sought, successfully, a cautious détente with a chastened Catholic Church. Old political rancours faded (or were driven underground); the central government increasingly controlled elections, while repressing armed dissent; and Díaz ensured that no vigorous political parties would disturb the emergent 'Pax Porfiriana' ('Porfirian peace'). 'Mucha administración y poca política'—'lots of administration and not too much politics'—became the watchword of the regime.

## The Porfirian economy

Now, Mexico belatedly entered the global division of labour as a supplier of raw materials and importer of capital (though not of labour: unlike Brazil or Argentina, Mexico could never attract mass migration from Europe, since the material incentives were lacking). Silver mining rapidly revived, but was now supplemented by new industrial mineral exports—copper, zinc, lead—which met the demand of the Second Industrial Revolution in Europe and the US. Agricultural exports, many of them 'non-traditional', also expanded: coffee, cotton, cacao, timber, vanilla, and later rubber. In Yucatán production of henequen—the fibrous extract of the agave plant—experienced a boom, thanks to the voracious demand of the American Midwest for sacking and binding twine. Thus, after a long pause, Mexico was integrated into circuits of world trade; global integration came later than in many Latin American countries and, in consequence, was the more rapid and destabilizing.

Integration would not have happened without the favourable political circumstances of the Porfiriato and the advent of foreign investment, which the regime sedulously encouraged. Díaz cut the military budget and switched expenditure to economic goals (such as railway subsidies, port installations, and telegraphs). By balancing the budget, his administration restored the country's credit and could borrow at increasingly favourable rates. By the 1900s, when, as a further token of financial prudence, the Mexican peso was placed on the Gold Standard, Mexico could borrow at 5 per cent and the long-standing Finance Minister, José Yves Limantour, enjoyed a charmed reputation in international business and banking circles.

Meanwhile, foreign direct investment, initially mostly European, later increasingly North American, flowed into mining (and later oil), banking, commercial agriculture, stockraising, public utilities (gas, electricity, water, trams), and some manufacturing sectors, especially textiles. But the key sector was the new railway network, built at a brisk clip during the 1880s and 1890s, which linked Mexico City to both the Atlantic port of Veracruz and the northern border, where three trunklines connected to the new North American transcontinental system. US capital predominated in the north, European in the centre; and the regime was careful to play off rival foreign interests, seeking to maximize Mexican advantage and to ensure that, in particular, the burgeoning US did not acquire overwhelming influence south of the Río Grande. Meanwhile, the railways dramatically lowered transport costs, making possible production—of both minerals and agricultural products—on an unprecedented scale.

The old 'black legend' of the Porfiriato—the stock-in-trade of the victorious revolutionaries—held that Díaz had betrayed both his country and his liberal-patriotic lineage by kowtowing to foreign interests. He was a *vendepatrias* (a 'seller-out of his country') who ensured that Mexico became 'the mother of foreigners and the step-mother of Mexicans'. The term 'Científico', denoting Díaz's inner coterie of advisers, became a term of opprobrium. This was effective political propaganda, but a serious distortion of history. Díaz had few illusions about the US and sought to attract American trade and investment without succumbing to American tutelage (as Cuba did after 1898). He and his advisers, notably Limantour, sought to balance rival foreign interests and to ensure that they worked to Mexico's advantage, at least as they, the Porfirian policy-makers, conceived it. *Desarrollo hacia afuera*—'outward-led development'—was the norm throughout Latin America in this period, when world trade was booming and foreign investment abundant. And, by the official standards of the day, the Porfirian regime was strikingly successful: railway mileage increased from virtually none to 15,000 miles; foreign direct investment grew more than thirty-fold; exports quadrupled and GNP nearly tripled. Not surprisingly, Díaz became a darling of foreigner observers, investors, and diplomats, who lyrically compared him to Moses, Alexander the Great, Cromwell, Bismarck, and Lincoln.

There is no doubt that, by premising his project of national development on sustained foreign investment, Díaz encouraged a form of external 'dependency'. By the 1900s, when the regime had lost its old populist reputation and opposition was mounting, Díaz—or, more likely, Limantour—was at pains to reassure foreign markets; the need to maintain Mexico's credit dictated currency policy, possibly to the detriment of domestic living standards. On the other hand, Limantour deployed the power of the state to create a national railway merger and considered ways of both regulating and taxing the crucial mining sector. Furthermore, 'dependency' did not stymie Mexico's manufacturing industry (as some have argued). *Desarrollo hacia afuera* was quite compatible with domestic industrialization, especially from the 1890s. The textile industry burgeoned, light industry flourished in Mexico City, while in the north-east the booming city of Monterrey, dominated by its powerful business elite, pioneered Mexico's steel and cement production.

Thus, while some critics claimed that Díaz was subservient to foreign interests and, in response, raised the cry of 'Mexico for the Mexicans', they did not represent mainstream popular interests. Many of the rebels of 1910–11, such as the Zapatistas of Morelos, had scant contact with the big—chiefly British, French, and American—foreign interests (the local landlords being Mexican or, occasionally, Spanish); in the north, many rebels were familiar with those interests, but saw them as vital players in both local economies and Mexico's national project of development. Pancho Villa had worked for foreign companies, proving himself to be a capable foreman; and, when he rose to become the chief caudillo (warlord) of the north, his relations with the American mining, cattle, and railway companies were generally cordial. There was no desire to erect Chinese walls against foreign influence; and, unlike the Chinese Boxers, the revolutionaries were in no sense violent xenophobes.

## The social impact: the Porfirian state

However, the Porfirian pattern of development did have a decisive—and negative—effect on Mexican society, especially rural society (where over 70 per cent of the population lived). Two related trends were crucial: the strengthening of the state and the commercialization of agriculture. A stronger state was essential in order to promote political stability, business confidence, and the fabled Pax Porfiriana. And certainly the mature Porfirian state was stronger than any that had governed the country since independence. It was solvent; it faced no major political challenges, armed or peaceful; and it controlled a slimmed-down but loyal army, which benefited from up-to-date weaponry, foreign training, and the enormous advantages of railways and telegraphs.

In addition, Díaz could rely on the rural police, a mounted corps fancifully compared to their Royal Canadian counterparts, whose public image—one of brisk efficiency and macho gallantry—was at odds with their actual practice, which involved graft, nepotism, and a complacent preference for the quiet life of *cuartel* and cantina (barracks and bar). But the rural police—the *rurales*—were fully capable of repressing scattered popular protests—on the part of aggrieved peasants, newly organized workers, or the occasional outspoken political dissident. Given its new technology, the army could also outgun any potential rebel, so rebellions came to seem futile; and, even when they occurred—for example, in the remote extremities of the north-west and south-east, where Yaqui and Maya Indian insurgencies were long-standing, the state emerged triumphant, albeit at the cost of behaving like a repressive and even racist colonial regime.

By the 1900s, even as discontent mounted, events seemed to prove that successful armed revolt was out of the question. In 1901, a local political squabble in the state of San Luis Potosí gave rise to a broadly based liberal movement which questioned the (unconstitutional) resurgence of the Catholic Church and called on Díaz to govern democratically according to the provisions of the 1857 (liberal) Constitution. The potential for active political opposition became apparent; but Díaz, rather than bow to liberal demands (thus making a reality of the 'public transcript'—the official discourse—of his regime) chose to harass, arrest, and exile his opponents, choking off the last best chance of democratic reform steered from above. The liberal leaders, exiled to the US, consorted with American radicals and veered to the left; the 1906 programme of the Partido Liberal Mexicano (PLM, Mexican Liberal Party) was as much anarcho-syndicalist as it was liberal, as well as being robustly nationalist. But a radical minority in exile could not threaten the regime; when the PLM attempted revolts on Mexican soil, in 1906 and 1908, they were easily put down; and the disorganized mainstream opposition within Mexico showed no desire to take the risky road of armed revolt.

For the first time since independence, the state was sufficiently strong to defy opposition challenges and its writ ran further than that of any previous national government. Díaz controlled the state governors who were allowed considerable licence—to feather their nests and preserve their regional political dominance—so long as they respected the power of 'the centre'. In many states, enduring oligarchies emerged, combining political and economic power, beholden to 'the centre' and often indifferent to popular interests. Indeed that indifference became more pronounced with time, as the old liberal veterans of the 1860s and 1870s (of whom Díaz was one) gave way to a new generation of well-heeled civilian oligarchs, products of the Pax Porfiriana, believers in the positivistic philosophy of the regime, and disdainful of the disenfranchised popular masses. A classic case was the state of Morelos, south of Mexico City, where the old veteran Manuel Alarcón was succeeded, as governor, by the 'prissy dukeling' Pablo Escandón, the young scion of a wealthy landed family, educated at an English Catholic school, who arrogantly ignored peasant—and 'Indian'—protest. The regime's capacity to mediate, to channel mounting discontent, thus atrophied.

Below the state governors, a lower tier of authority consisted of the *jefes políticos* (political bosses), appointed officials responsible for policing, public order, and general political surveillance. The *jefes políticos* reported up to Díaz and were the eyes, ears, and arm of the state; in their long shadow, local municipal democracy wilted; and popular protest, when it broke out in 1910, was frequently directed against these local agents of Porfirian power. The entrenched state oligarchies—such as the Creel/Terrazas faction in Chihuahua—were also bitterly unpopular; while Díaz, though he remained, to the end, the spider at the centre of the web, was sufficiently remote—perhaps, also, sufficiently patriarchal in bearing and reputation—to escape the worst opprobrium.

Meanwhile, communities and regions that, in the past, had had tenuous contact with the central government, now fell firmly under its control (or, at least, that of its appointed minions). The balance of power shifted decisively from the provinces to 'the centre', as it was known. Taxation, political appointments, and social control became more onerous and oppressive. Historically, northern Mexico had developed autonomously of the centre—combating the so-called *indios bárbaros* ('barbarous Indians') of the region (Apaches and Comanches), trading and smuggling across the US border, and building a dynamic economy based on mining and livestock. Northerners tended to see themselves as more progressive and go-ahead and they resented the distant but capricious authority of the capital. In particular, northern *serranos*—highland people, who inhabited the long chain of the Sierra Madre mountains—chafed at the growing authority of both Mexico City and provincial capitals like Chihuahua City, which was controlled by a particularly powerful politico-economic clique, the Creel/Terrazas faction.

While such *serrano*/autonomist sentiments were unusually strong in the north, especially the highland north, they were also to be found throughout Mexico, wherever traditional local autonomy had to yield to the burgeoning authority of the Porfirian state: in the Puebla and Oaxaca highlands; on the inland frontier of Yucatán; and in bucolic communities in the centre-west, such as San José de Gracia (Michoacan), where dislike of the central state was enhanced by Catholic suspicions of Díaz—a known, if perhaps an apostate, liberal.

Though ostensibly strong in terms of its stability and reach, the Porfirian state was weak in respect of resources and, even more, popular legitimacy (a point to stress, since it suggests important contrasts with the later revolutionary state). Dependent on foreign trade taxes, the state had a slim, albeit stable, income: it was solvent, but it took less than 5 per cent of GDP in the form of revenue, a paltry $4 (US) per capita. Its expenditure was largely limited to 'administrative' items: paying the army and the modest state bureaucracy while, above all, servicing the foreign debt.

The state also undertook, or subsidized, key infrastructural investment: in ports, telegraphs, and, above all, railways. But its role was limited to creating the conditions within which domestic and foreign capitalists could prosper. Above all, the state played a minimal role when it came to social policy: basic education was supplied, patchily at best, by the cash-starved municipalities (so Mexico's literacy rate hovered around 20 per cent); and virtually no attempts were made to protect, uplift, or improve the lot of Mexico's workers and peasants. At most, late in the regime's life, some concern was felt for the so-called 'social question' (shorthand for urban squalor and working-class protest), and Díaz made half-hearted efforts to mediate in the mounting industrial disputes of the 1900s.

## The social impact: organized labour and the peasantry

In two such disputes, however, the state showed its true colours. In 1906, when workers at the American-owned Cananea copper mine in Sonora, close to the Arizona border, went on strike, the conflict turned violent and Mexican police collaborated with American company guards and Arizona Rangers in repressing the workers, killing some twenty. A year later, the principal textile zone of central Mexico—the Puebla/Orizaba region, east of the capital—was also affected by strikes, protests, and lockouts. Despite mediating in the conflict, Díaz finally sent in the troops and, in the ensuing repression, over a hundred workers were killed or executed. The 1907 depression combined with this draconian response to stifle working-class protest. But the potential for protest remained and the workers, though far fewer than the majority peasantry, were strategically placed in the major cities and in key sectors of the economy (the textile factories, railways, ports, mines, and oil camps), alert for an opportunity to press their interests. Thus, right up to the revolutionary debacle of 1910–11, the regime remained committed to a policy of top-down social control, spurning both enlightened social reform and effective political representation. In the eyes of most Mexicans, therefore, the state existed in order to control and if necessary repress; it increasingly lacked both social penetration (the ability to put down roots in society) and political legitimacy (the capacity to elicit voluntary obedience from its citizens).

Worse, the regime's agrarian policies stoked the fires of peasant discontent—in a country where some three-quarters of the population were rural and poor. Mexico's integration into world markets spurred demand for agricultural exports, already mentioned; meanwhile, the national market for both basic consumer goods (corn, beans, chile, wheat, sugar, and pulque—the alcoholic drink of the common people) and also industrial raw materials (cotton, timber, leather) burgeoned, to the benefit of the landlord class. The railways, which underpinned the power of the Porfirian state, also tied myriad local markets into regional and national networks; land values and agrarian profits rose; and the owners of haciendas (large estates), who had for generations complained of inadequate transport and scant demand, now entered a *belle époque* of profitable expansion. The haciendas were—in many cases—ancient creations of the colony; but it required the Pax Porfiriana and the stimulus of demand to turn them into dynamic expansionist enterprises.

Again, the state played a key role. Since the colony, the hacienda had coexisted with the peasant (sometimes also the Indian) village; while, between these two key rural antagonists, stood a class of middling farmers (rancheros). Hacienda–village conflict was old, but had been constrained by the flaccidity of the rural economy, as well as the threat of peasant protest, which historically deterred landlords (and the state) from pushing the peasants too hard. Through much of the 19th century recurrent warfare—which often involved peasant levies—constrained hacienda expansion, while affording the peasantry substantial bargaining power. Most villages were thoroughly familiar with the market and with private property; they combined freehold property with corporate (community-owned) fields, pasture, and woods; they often rented or share cropped hacienda land, or worked as labourers on hacienda demesnes.

But this rough equilibrium, the product of economic sluggishness and socio-political stand-off, broke down during the Porfiriato. Under Juárez, the liberals had legislated to turn corporate property into freehold, thus to create a vigorous ranchero class. Though some pockets of ranchero farming prospered, the liberals' Jeffersonian vision largely failed. Under Díaz, as peace bolstered business confidence and market demand quickened, hacendados—and some rancheros—took advantage of liberal laws to appropriate village land; thus, peasant villages—like Anenecuilco, in Morelos, the ancestral home of the Zapata family—came under increased pressure. At the same time, the regime sold off vast areas of public land (*baldíos*), in the hope of promoting immigration, investment, and development; but the chief beneficiaries were, again, the big landowners, especially those politically close to the regime.

Landlords now had greater incentives to acquire—whether by legal purchase or shady dealing—the historic patrimony of peasant villages; in the process, they 'freed' the peasants from their means of subsistence, obliging them to switch from independent subsistence farming to tenancy, sharecropping, or wage-labour on the expanding estates. Since, at the same time, moderate population growth (1.3 per cent per year) swelled the rural population, the labour supply grew and real wages declined—a trend evident at least from the mid-1890s. Furthermore, integration into world markets made Mexico—for the first time—seriously vulnerable to the vicissitudes of the global business cycle. In 1907, recession in the US depressed demand for Mexican exports and generated severe unemployment, especially in the north. This was a short-term shock, a conjunctural crisis which affected material living standards in the more commercialized sectors of the economy; but more serious still was the structural tension engendered by extensive peasant dispossession (or, if you prefer, 'proletarianisation'), which threatened not only material hardship but also a loss of community autonomy and identity. In Morelos, where the sugar planters systematically squeezed the ancient peasant villages of the region, the ruins of lost villages decayed amid the lush field of sugarcane which now blanketed the state, mute testimony to the 'planters' progress' which seemed to be carrying all before it. And Morelos epitomized, in extreme form, a shift in power and resources which affected much of rural Mexico.

As already suggested, the impact of these agrarian changes varied by region. And Mexico, being a vast, highly diverse country, can be endlessly subdivided into regions. The simplest typology involves just three macro-regions. In the north, pockets of agrarian dispossession—in La Laguna, the Yaqui Valley, or the foothills of the Sierra Madre—existed within a more broadly commercial economy, based on mining and livestock, now highly vulnerable to external shocks like the 1907 recession. Thus, in the north we see both traditional peasant protest—for example, the renewed rebellion of the Yaqui Indians of Sonora—as well as broader discontent which united the urban middle class and the growing working class (miners, railwaymen, muleteers, smugglers, and bandits). In central Mexico, where the bulk of the population resided, the classic confrontation of expansionist haciendas and ancient peasant villages was widespread: now, thanks to the conflictual process of Porfirian economic growth, an old story was played out with unprecedented severity, since both economic livelihood and communal existence were at stake. Both regions would play a salient role in the armed revolution.

The south (more strictly, the south-east, from the state of Oaxaca down to Chiapas and Yucatán) proved less revolutionary: not because times were good and people were happy, but because the apparatus of social control was stronger, hence discontent could be stifled. The south was the poorest, most illiterate and Indian part of the country. Like the centre, it housed a dense Indian peasantry—especially in the southern highlands and the hot lowlands of Yucatán—as well as an aggressive planter class, engaged in dynamic cash-crop production: tobacco in Oaxaca, henequen in Yucatán, coffee and logging in Chiapas. Cities were fewer and smaller, hence middle-class opposition was weaker.

The dominant landlord class, bent on exports (and including European and American planters), resorted to harsh measures to acquire labour—largely Indian labour—from the southern villages. If cash incentives proved inadequate, the planters—and their allies in the local and state governments—relied on coercive forms of peonage, whereby workers were snared in debt or simply dragooned into work on the henequen, cacao, coffee, and tobacco plantations of the south. Perhaps the worst oppression—a form of quasi-slavery—occurred in the Chiapas highlands, where logging companies practised a form of ruthless predatory exploitation, indifferent to both human and environmental costs. Yet the south was not notably revolutionary: the carapace of social control proved too strong, the protests of Indians and peons too weak and sporadic. Revolution would not come to the south until northern proconsuls and their forces arrived in 1914, determined to incorporate this—as they saw it—benighted and backward region into the revolutionary mainstream.

## Political sclerosis and presidential succession

While successful by its own 'Científico' lights and lauded by foreign observers, the Porfirian political economy thus involved two related features which, over time, proved provocative and destabilizing: the creation of a strong authoritarian state (which denied representation and lacked legitimacy) and the pursuit of export-led development premised on rapid agrarian commercialization, to the marked detriment of the rural majority. While similar features can be discerned throughout Latin America at the time, in Mexico the process was unusually rapid and concentrated (the work of a single generation); and it impacted upon communities, especially rural communities, which had a long history of popular mobilization (not least, in the patriotic war against the French in the 1860s). Initially a popular and successful liberal hero, Díaz became increasingly detached from his supporters, reliant on Científico counsel, and unable to control the process of economic development he had helped initiate. Born in 1830, he was, by 1910, an old man, whose powers were in decline. Even when he attempted to rein in the provocative expansion of commercial landlords—for example, at the agrarian trouble-spot of Tamazunchale in the Huasteca—he found that his powers of mediation could not halt the headlong advance of land expropriation and concentration.

Meanwhile, within the narrow ranks of the Porfirian oligarchy, middle-aged aspirants for power began to jockey for the succession: in particular, Finance Minister Limantour, the guarantor of foreign business confidence, contested with General Bernardo Reyes, who enjoyed support in the economically buoyant north-east, and in the ranks of the army and its reserve militia (which Reyes had founded). But Díaz was loath to relinquish power. He played his rivals off against each other and, when a vice-presidency was instituted in 1904, he ensured that the appointee, Ramón Corral, was an unpopular figure, lacking support, thus posing no threat to Díaz's personal authority. No efforts were made to institutionalize the regime: Díaz was re-elected president—in 1900 and 1904—by means of managed elections in which fly-by-night political parties existed solely to propose and applaud his re-election. But when a presidential election loomed again in 1910, a quite different scenario emerged, which took the regime by surprise and provided the opening act of the Revolution.

If the combustible fuel of the Revolution thus derived from socio-economic—especially agrarian—tensions, the timing of the explosion obeyed a political rationale: the lead-up to the 1910 presidential election, which would inaugurate a six-year presidential term which Díaz could hardly be expected to survive. (In fact he died in 1915, in exile in France.) While oligarchic insiders jockeyed for power, seeking the president's favour, a broader political opposition now mobilized, chiefly in Mexico's burgeoning cities, calling for free elections, party competition, and a democratic succession. Essentially, the opposition sought to make a reality of the liberal Constitution of 1857—which still prevailed (in theory), and still stirred strong positive sentiments, even though Díaz had systematically traduced it in practice. In 1908 Díaz unwisely and perhaps unwittingly gave encouragement to the nascent opposition, declaring to an American journalist that Mexico was now ready for free democratic elections. His motives have been much debated; perhaps he wanted to smoke out the opposition; possibly he fell victim to a palace conspiracy; certainly he wanted to please American opinion. At any rate, now old and out of touch, he misjudged the consequences, since his invitation to political contestation was taken at face value by citizens who sought to make a reality of their paper constitutional rights.

## The rise of opposition

Those citizens spanned a wide range of classes and sectors. The middle class—white-collar workers, professionals, and smaller businessmen—had grown along with the cities and the deepening of the market. These were literate people, who read the press, knew their Mexican history, and had a grasp of global news. Many harked back to the glorious old liberal-patriotic tradition of Juárez which, it was reasonably alleged, Díaz had abandoned in the interests of authoritarian power and skewed economic development. (The comparison may have flattered Juárez, but it was a cogent criticism of Díaz.) Such people also pointed to the advance of democracy in Europe (Republican France being the preferred model), in the US (where the Progressive movement was in full swing), and elsewhere in Latin America (notably Argentina).

For all its material advance, Mexico seemed mired in a retrograde personal dictatorship.

If the literate and articulate urban middle class tended to dominate the incipient opposition of 1908–10, it did not lack for popular allies. The Mexican working class—both industrial workers and the more numerous artisan class—were strongly drawn to liberalism, which promised them representation and civic rights, while appealing to their staunch patriotic sentiments—liberalism having fused with patriotism in the crucible of the French Intervention. As already mentioned, patriotism did not mean Boxerish xenophobia but, given that many companies and bosses were foreign (Cananea and Río Blanco, scenes of recent repression, were American and French companies respectively), liberalism exerted an additional appeal among Mexican workers. Many of the latter were literate; in particular, the urban artisans prided themselves on a measure of book-learning; they knew Mexican history (typically from a liberal/Juarista perspective), they eagerly read the 'penny press' (popular newspapers, aimed at the workers, notable for their acerbic caricatures), and, like aspiring artisans elsewhere in Catholic Europe or Latin America, they often displayed a robust anticlericalism.

The cities tended to be the focus of liberal opposition, but the countryside was by no means inert or detached. The liberal tradition had deep roots in rural communities and families (including prominent revolutionaries-to-be like Zapata, Obregón, and Cárdenas) and, while it was harder to mobilize in scattered rural communities, a sequence of contested state elections in 1908, 1909, and 1910 showed that country people were also keen to back opposition candidates against the official nominees. Central political control began to slip from the hands of the regime.

Meanwhile, popular demands from below conspired with divisions with the narrow Porfirian elite. General Bernardo Reyes, a suitably macho military figure with a veneer of progressivism, emerged as the figurehead of the opposition. But Reyes was Díaz's creature, ill-suited to lead a genuine political insurgency, and when Díaz sent him on a prolonged international mission (in effect, a decorous exile), he meekly complied. The vacuum at the top was now filled by another elite figure, though of a very different kind: Francisco Madero, a short, balding landlord and businessman, scion of one of the richest families of northern Mexico, foreign educated, a devotee of spiritism and homoeopathic medicine, but a genuine idealist who sought—by peaceful persuasion—to make a reality of Mexico's liberal-democratic tradition. Advocating *sufragio efectivo, no re-elección* ('a real vote and no re-election'), Madero's Anti-reelectionist Party called for free elections in 1910 (in which Díaz could himself participate) (see Figure 1).

Their programme was quintessentially liberal, political, and moderate: Madero, like many of his supporters, was well aware of

1. **Anti-reelectionists—supporters of Francisco Madero—march in support of 'A Real Vote and No Re-election', in opposition to President Porfirio Díaz, 1910: typically, the scene is urban and the marchers are a mix of middle- and working-class men.**

broader socio-economic grievances (the plight of urban workers, land hunger, the repression of the Yaqui Indians), but he favoured narrowly political solutions. Free elections, as Madero told the textile workers of Orizaba, would enable them to voice their grievances; but he did not offer them anything resembling socialism, still less social revolution.

Díaz underestimated Madero, while Madero's own family spurned his quixotic political crusade. But it prospered. Copying the methods of US campaigning, Madero barnstormed the country by train, addressing mass meetings, distributing lapel buttons, attracting large and enthusiastic crowds. The regime was rattled: no such challenge had been mounted in a generation of Porfirian rule. The authorities tried to beat Madero at his own game, but official rallies lacked appeal and tended to backfire. So the regime resorted to what it knew best—repression. Anti-reelectionist clubs were closed down, rallies were broken up, and opposition leaders—including Madero himself—were arrested. By the summer of 1910, as Mexico prepared to celebrate the centennial of its independence from Spain, it seemed that the regime had turned the corner. In June, Díaz was re-elected in an anodyne, stage-managed poll. Madero languished in gaol. Three months later, the Centennial went ahead with much self-congratulatory celebration and glad-handing. A German diplomat confidently reassured Berlin that 'I consider general revolution to be out of the question, as does public opinion and the press.' He was not the last foreign observer seriously to misread Mexican reality.

# Chapter 3
# The Madero revolt and regime (1910–1913)

## From ballots to bullets

However, diplomats confined to the hothouse of Mexico City had very little idea of what was going on in the vast sprawling spaces of provincial Mexico. Madero's political campaign of 1909–10 had given hope to the many Mexicans, especially rural Mexicans, who resented the political bossism and economic abuses of the Porfiriato. Having promised a free election, Díaz had reneged: the door to peaceful electoral reform was slammed shut. The middle class of the major cities saw little point in persisting in quixotic opposition: they risked reprisals and had their careers and businesses to consider. Furthermore they were ill-suited to armed revolution: penned in the cities, they lacked guns, machetes, mounts, mobility, boltholes, and, perhaps most important of all, the experience and tradition of guerrilla warfare. All recent revolts had been readily put down. But Madero, quirky and quixotic, reached the inevitable conclusion that peaceful politicking had failed: he jumped bail and fled to the US, calling for an armed insurrection to begin on 20 November.

Now, the Revolution entered its armed phase, which demanded a significant change of personnel. The urban middle classes retired to the wings; so, too, did the urban working class who, by and large, were similarly ill-suited to violent insurrection (remember the repression of Cananea and Río Blanco). The cities were closely controlled by the Porfirian authorities: indeed, the first shots of the Revolution were fired, two days ahead of schedule, when police pre-emptively raided the house of Aquiles Serdán, a Maderista leader in the city of Puebla, starting a gun battle which led to Serdán's death. The Revolution had its first heroic martyr; and—confounding the old national stereotype—the Mexicans began their Revolution two days early. In most towns and cities the official crackdown on dissidents was similarly successful. To many, it seemed that yet another futile rebellion had been nipped in the bud. But then, initially in the north, isolated revolts broke out, defied official repression, and began to prosper.

The first major guerrilla 'foco' (centre) was established in the mountains of western Chihuahua, in rough country, where rebellion had flared up in the 1890s, where the radical PLM enjoyed support, and where the local population—cowboys, muleteers, miners, bandits, and peasant villagers—were known to be redoubtable fighters, well versed in riding, shooting, and living off the land. Their fathers and grandfathers had fought the Apaches and Comanches, and the tradition of frontier fighting had not been entirely extinguished by the Pax Porfiriana. The first popular leader to emerge was Pascual Orozco, a muleteer in his late twenties, scion of a well-known family of poor-to-middling status, who, like many of his people, nursed grievances against the local authorities. Indeed, western Chihuahua was notorious for its hated local bosses (caciques), who were cogs in the state political machine, run by the powerful Creel/Terrazas faction. One final factor was relevant: the proximity of the US border enabled the pioneer rebels to import arms and ammunition (illegally, and necessarily in small quantities); while the mining camps and cattle spreads of the north afforded resources (including dynamite) which could be appropriated for the revolutionary cause.

If Chihuahua enjoyed particular advantages, similar guerrilla movements soon sprang up throughout northern and central

Mexico (the south, in contrast, remained relatively quiet). The pattern was similar: small bands of young men, often connected by ties of kinship, took to the hills, launching hit-and-run raids against haciendas and army detachments, their first priority being the acquisition of guns, ammunition, and horses. In the gestation of popular revolt, both contextual and causal factors were important. That is, successful revolt depended on both capacity (organization, arms, local knowledge, and contacts) and grievances (oppressive authorities, expansionist landlords). While agrarian grievances were apparent in pockets of the north—in the Yaqui Valley, the cotton country of La Laguna, and the state of Durango—they were more frequent in the densely populated regions of central Mexico, where commercial haciendas had expanded at the expense of ancient, sometimes Indian, peasant communities.

In the state of Morelos, where sugar plantations had prospered during the Porfiriato, local squabbles had simmered for decades, as aggrieved villagers protested, litigated, and finally took up arms. For them, Madero was a congenial, if distant, figurehead; his call to national revolution legitimized a local cause; and, while his invocation of Juárez and the old liberal tradition carried weight (since many of these communities and families had fought for the liberals in the past), the Morelos rebels essentially mounted their own autonomous rebellion under the broad umbrella of Maderismo. The same was true of many revolts which sprang up during 1910–11: they obeyed local concerns and were led by local leaders who shared the grievances of their followers and had the capacity to rally them in improvised guerrilla campaigns.

By spring 1911 such minor rebellions had spread across much of northern and central Mexico. The Porfirian regime faced an unprecedented armed challenge. Though slimmed down by Díaz, the Federal Army was fully capable of holding the major towns, where its advantages in weaponry (Mauser rifles, machine guns, and artillery) were overwhelming. But the countryside was slipping from the state's control and the legendary *rurales*, who cut fine figures in the eyes of impressionable Mexico City tourists, proved utterly incapable of policing the countryside as they were supposed to. By virtue of their speed, elusiveness, and overwhelming popular support, the rebels could evade pursuit and build up their forces piecemeal. This was a classic case of 'asymmetrical' warfare: a static well-armed conventional force confronting highly mobile—but poorly armed—popular rebels.

Madero, the nominal leader of the Revolution, spent the early months of the insurrection in the US. Some have claimed that US interests—the US government and/or big US companies—backed the Revolution in the hope of toppling Díaz. Like most conspiracy theories, this cannot be definitively refuted (if the conspiracy is a good one, it leaves few traces). But the claim makes little sense. The Taft administration—a conservative Republican administration headed by a legalistic president—had good relations with Díaz and, in confronting the turmoil to the south, it followed legal norms: there were no grounds for arresting Madero unless he actively led an armed incursion across the border. US companies could, of course, clandestinely fund foreign rebellions if they chose; but it is difficult to see why they would choose to do so in this case. They had done well under Díaz's rule and, even if some US interests resented the alleged preference shown to the British entrepreneur Weetman Pearson (Lord Cowdray), it would have been a rash and risky business to plan the ouster of the long-standing president in the expectation of some hypothetical benefit. Perhaps some minor foreign (not necessarily American) interests put speculative money into Madero's pocket; but all the evidence suggests that the financing of the Revolution was scanty and depended on the personal finances of those involved (Madero himself was rich), as well as the resources raised, on the ground in Mexico, by the rebel forces. And this meant, of course, that they were poorly armed, short of ammunition, and compelled to face the Federals' Mausers with, at best, Winchester rifles—hunting weapons which soon overheated in a sustained firefight.

As the Revolution spread, it became clear that Madero could not remain in the US: the Díaz government clamoured for his arrest which, sooner or later, seemed likely; and, as the nominal leader of the Revolution, he had to exert his authority over the fast-growing but scattered and uncoordinated rebel forces. In February he crossed into Chihuahua, putting himself at the head of the largest rebel force, of perhaps 500 men. An ill-advised confrontation with Federal Army forces at Casas Grandes confirmed that the rebels could not face Díaz's professional army in open battle. The guerrilla war went on; meanwhile, in Mexico City, the vested interests of the old regime began to react to this unprecedented situation. Díaz sacked a few unpopular governors and made emollient noises. But it was too little too late. His key allies and advisers looked to save their own political skins, and to maintain the structure of the old regime, even if it meant ditching Díaz himself.

In April, as Madero mustered his rag-tag army on the outskirts of the northern border city of Ciudad Juárez, the government agreed to talks. But Díaz refused to resign, as the rebels demanded, and the talks broke down. Fearful that an attack on Juárez would produce casualties in neighbouring El Paso, Madero prudently ordered his army to retreat to the south. But his authority was tenuous and his plebeian lieutenants, spoiling for a fight, disobeyed and began to blast their way into the city, using improvised dynamite bombs against vulnerable adobe walls. Soon, the city was theirs, the Federal garrison had surrendered, and a major border port was in revolutionary hands. Talks were resumed and Díaz agreed to resign, in favour of an interim president, while Madero undertook to demobilize his forces and await the outcome of fresh presidential elections.

## The Madero administrations: the travails of liberalism

This, the Treaty of Ciudad Juárez, ended the Maderista revolution as well as the Porfirian regime. It has been strongly criticized as a premature capitulation, which allowed the substance of the old regime—the army, officialdom, and political elite—to persist, while stopping the Revolution in its tracks. The criticism is valid, but, just as the Porfirian elite saw the advantages of compromise, so, too, did Madero and some fellow-leaders of the Revolution. A humanitarian, Madero wanted to avoid further bloodshed; he also realized that, if they were to seize major cities from Federal hands (as they had Juárez), it would require extensive and costly fighting; and he was aware that, throughout northern and central Mexico, the partial collapse of the old regime threatened a descent into chaos. Sizeable rebel forces now prowled the countryside, threatening incursions into the cities. Aggrieved peasants were occupying disputed land. In isolated cities, food prices rose and the urban poor grew restive. Eventually riots broke out: in northern mining towns like Concepción del Oro, where local officials were butchered; in the big cities of the Bajío, home of a near-destitute artisan class; and in the cotton-country metropolis of Torreón where, unusually, the rebel forces joined with the local mob to loot and murder, the chief victims being the city's Chinese community. This was not the decorous liberal-democratic revolution which Madero and his *bien-pensant* allies had envisaged; hence their readiness to do a swift deal with the old regime.

But the deal rankled, especially with rebel leaders—like Orozco in the north or Zapata in the centre—who now led sizeable forces and could smell victory. The later history of the Revolution would amply confirm that the opinion of local military leaders was crucial to any durable political settlement. But Madero feared anarchy and favoured peace and order. He also too readily assumed that the likes of Zapata and Orozco—young, uneducated, plebeian warlords-in-the-making—were unsuitable for high office (again, the later history of the Revolution proved otherwise). At the cost of much popular dissent and disaffection, the peace treaty held and an interim president—the conservative Catholic Francisco León de la Barra—took office, pending a presidential election in October which, predictably, Madero comfortably won, taking office a month later. Over the summer, however, the strains of the peace settlement became more acute. Interim President de la Barra threw his weight behind conservative elite interests who clung to power, while the 'Liberating Army' of the Revolution, hastily assembled during the winter and spring, was just as hastily demobilized and sent home. The first, short bout of civil war was over: it had ousted Díaz—who sailed into exile in France—and installed Madero as elected president. He could now implement his liberal-democratic political programme, but in testing circumstances, marked by mounting social and political tension.

## Opposition, Right and Left

Madero had promised 'a real vote and no re-election': a functioning liberal democracy in accord with the 1857 Constitution. He was sincere, if naive, in pursuing these goals. But he faced enormous obstacles. On the Right (to use convenient and conventional labels) he had to reckon with the elites of the old regime, whom the peace treaty had spared: the landlord class, foreign and Mexican business interests, the Porfirian bureaucracy, and, above all, the army. (The position of the Church was more ambiguous; however, the Catholic hierarchy, as we will see, feared the Revolution and gravitated into the conservative camp.) These were minority interests, but they had money, status, influence, and political access. Above all, they sought a return to the Porfiriato, by which they meant strong authoritarian government which would keep Mexico's insurgent plebs in check. With Díaz gone, they looked to leaders like Bernardo Reyes or Félix Díaz (the deposed president's nephew) to assume the Porfirian mantle.

On the Left, meanwhile, stood the forces who had brought Madero to power, but whom he had summarily sent home: popular leaders like Orozco and Zapata, backed by their popular levies; insurgent peasants who sought to recover their lost lands; an incipient working-class movement which, though it had not risen up en masse in 1910–11, now took advantage of the new regime to organize, strike, and press their claims through the ballot box; and radicals—including some of the old PLM veterans and their followers—who wanted to push the Revolution beyond the narrow confines of Maderista liberalism. Madero found himself marooned on a narrowing middle ground, threatened by a rising tide to both Right and Left (though his tendency, over time, was to shift to the Right, that is, to rely on the Federal Army to bolster his fragile presidency).

The threats from Right and Left were qualitatively different. The Right, as an elite minority, could deploy the 'weapons of the strong'—money, political contacts, the power of the conservative press; but the Right lacked a mass following and, when it came to the *ultima ratio* of armed force, it had but one weapon (albeit a potentially crucial one): the Federal Army, which Madero courted, funded, and even expanded. So long as the army remained guardedly loyal, Madero was safe from a top-down military coup; hence, attempts by conservative leaders like Reyes or Félix Díaz to oust the president by insurrectionary means failed miserably. But the army watched and waited. The Left, loosely defined, could count on ample popular support, as had the initial Revolution of 1910–11. Disappointed by the peace treaty and the rightward shift of the Madero regime, revolutionary leaders now resumed their rebellious ways, denouncing Madero's betrayal of their cause. Two major revolts broke out in 1911–12; both were, in essence, continuations of the initial insurgency of 1910–11.

In Morelos, Zapata resumed his agrarian struggle, proclaiming the Plan of Ayala, which would remain the Zapatista programme and banner for nearly a decade. It excoriated Madero, reiterated the old Maderista promise of free elections, but also provided for a distribution of land from hacienda to village. Initially quite moderate, the agrarian demands of the Zapatistas grew more radical as the Revolution progressed and the country became more politically polarized. Zapatismo soon spilled over from Morelos into neighbouring states in central Mexico; meanwhile, rebel forces elsewhere—the Cedillo brothers in San Luis, insurgent Yaqui Indian in Sonora—seconded the Zapatista demand for land reform. Rooted in their peasant villages, fighting a classic guerrilla war, the Zapatistas were redoubtable opponents (see Figure 2). Madero, like a good hand-wringing liberal, lamented the need for harsh measures, but he unleashed the Federal Army on Morelos, where it adopted all the tactics typical of counter-insurgency, familiar from the Boer war and Spanish campaigns in insurgent Cuba: shooting prisoners, razing villages, and 'concentrating' the civilian population.

Morelos suffered; but Zapatismo proved inextinguishable. The fighting ebbed and flowed. Tied to their villages, the Zapatistas tended to campaign during the winter, roughly November–April; when the summer rains came, planting and harvesting took priority and the fighting ebbed, encouraging the Federal Army to claim, spuriously, that Zapatismo was a spent force. In nearby Mexico City, the conservative press, when it was not lampooning

2. Zapatista forces from southern Mexico, with accompanying soldadera.

President Madero, treated its readers to spine-chilling stories of Zapatista rapine. In fact, the rapine was largely the work of the Federal Army.

Zapatismo thus became the pre-eminent peasant and agrarian movement of central Mexico. In the north, a more serious challenge arose when Pascual Orozco declared against the Madero government early in 1912, alleging betrayal of the revolutionary cause, calling for social reform, and carrying with him many of the northern veterans of 1910–11. Orozquismo was thus a popular, radical, and nationalist movement which, unlike Zapatismo, benefited from ample regional resources as well as access to the US border. However, in a bizarre twist not unusual in the history of revolutions, disaffected members of the old Chihuahua elite, aggrieved at their loss of political power, threw in their lot with the rebellion, in the hope of overthrowing Madero and his regional representative, the reformist Governor Abraham González.

A short-lived marriage of convenience, this union of popular rebels and conservative counter-revolutionary elites was more feasible in the north—where popular motives were mixed and leaders like Orozco could be seduced by elite blandishments—than in central Mexico, where the weight of village tradition and the overriding goal of land reform deterred any such opportunistic alliance of Left and Right, plebs and patricians, against the beleaguered Centre. In Morelos, class divisions (accentuated by ethnicity) were too sharp: Zapata would no more ally with the sugar planters than they would ally with the swarthy 'bandit' who threatened their lives and livelihood.

As in 1910–11, the northern (Orozquista) revolution proved mobile and effective, winning a major battle at Rellano in March 1912. It seemed that the rebels might now advance on a panicky Mexico City. But Madero placed his faith in the Federal Army, commanded by a ruthless and experienced old general, Victoriano

Huerta, who, two months later, defeated the Orozquistas, his artillery taking a heavy toll. The rebels dispersed, now bent on raiding; and the chief politico-military threat to the Madero government was eliminated. The government survived, but it could not bring peace. The Zapatistas and other popular rebels remained active, chiefly in central Mexico.

In the south, too, the reverberations of Revolution were now felt. Following the fall of the Porfirian state, old disputes bubbled to the surface: if, in much of central Mexico, these derived from agrarian tensions (chiefly, the classic confrontation of village and hacienda), a secondary form of conflict involved battles for political pre-eminence between rival towns, cities, and regions. In Oaxaca—a sprawling, variegated, ethnically diverse southern state—the government in the Valley of Oaxaca struggled to impose its will on dissident communities both in the Mixtec highlands and down on the hot lowlands of the Isthmus of Tehuantepec. Further south, in Chiapas, a local civil war broke out, pitting the old clerical/conservative capital, San Cristóbal, against the new upstart—and liberal—city of Tuxtla Gutiérrez.

## The democratic experiment

With the glue of Porfirian rule removed, it seemed, the mosaic of national power created by Díaz was falling apart, as towns, villages, and localities sought to assert their autonomy against rivals, these assertions often involving class, ethnic, or ideological inflections. Madero, increasingly seen as an effete civilian, appeared unable to control the deteriorating situation; and many of his erstwhile middle-class supporters, who had hailed the new dawn of democracy in 1910, now gravitated to the Right, lamenting the breakdown of 'order and progress' and fearing for their own lives and livelihoods. Indeed, Madero himself, by bolstering the Federal Army and sanctioning repressive counter-insurgency campaigns in Morelos and elsewhere, encouraged this liberal apostasy.

Yet, at the same time, the president sought to institute a functioning democracy, as he had promised. Competitive elections were held; parties flourished; and 'mass publics' became involved in politics to a degree unknown under Díaz. At the same time, Madero allowed a much greater measure of press freedom (which much of the press used to snipe at the president). Mexico thus experienced a genuine, if partial, democratic *apertura* (opening). It was partial because, in a context of sustained social upheaval and even civil war, many regions—such as Morelos and Chihuahua—could hardly practise a limpid liberal democracy. In addition, the old Porfirian elite—still strong in the south, in particular—disdained democracy and strove to curtail mass political mobilization (even to the extent of eliminating dangerous popular leaders or outspoken journalists). In many cases, therefore, Maderista democracy failed to deliver, and appeared something of a sham. But in some parts of the country it functioned, after a fashion.

Three features of this incipient democracy deserve mention. First, in some states electoral politics assumed a class logic, as workers threw their weight behind preferred candidates. A key example was the oil port of Tampico, where a lively working class combined trade union activity with pragmatic politics, showing that the urban workers, even if they had not, in the main, taken up arms, were useful allies when it came to urban electoral politics. In the state of Tlaxcala, 'hyphenated' worker-peasants (who combined agricultural work with stints in the local textile factories) managed to elect one of their own to the state governorship, alarming the local landed elite. Though a minority in the land, organized labour thus displayed its political potential.

Second, in those regions where the Catholic Church was powerful—notably the centre-west (including the states of Jalisco, Guanajuato, Michoacan, and Aguascalientes)—a form of ideological politics arose, pitting liberals against political Catholics ('political Catholics' being those whose politics was premised on their Catholicism and who often took their cue from the *cura*—the parish priest). Liberal/Catholic conflict was nothing new in Mexican history, as I discuss in Chapter 6; but the initial Maderista revolution had avoided anticlericalism and Madero himself was a believer, if a rather unorthodox one. When, taking advantage of the democratic opening of 1911, a new Catholic Party (the PCN: Partido Católico Nacional) was formed, Madero welcomed it as a legitimate player in the new democratic game. The PCN was strong in the centre-west and soon acquired an important representation in the National Congress. While Madero applauded this outcome, some liberals, who carried the old anticlerical political gene, were alarmed and resisted. Catholics and liberals strenuously contested elections, sparred in the partisan press, and occasionally skirmished in the streets. As yet, this conflict could be seen as an inevitable squabble in the nursery of democracy. But it highlighted a crucial politico-cultural fault line which, before long, would become a broad and threatening abyss.

A final significant factor concerned the rise of what could be called 'populist' politics. Under Díaz, political office depended on the favour of the president or his senior cronies; some elected representatives had never set foot in the districts they 'represented'. The Maderista political *apertura* meant that popular support counted (e.g. in the cases of Tampico and Tlaxcala). As a result, a new brand of *político*, endowed with different traits, entered the political stage. We can take as a single example Alvaro Obregón, who will figure prominently in the following narrative. A small farmer from the go-ahead commercial north-western state of Sonora, Obregón had not—to his chagrin and regret—joined the Revolution in 1910–11. Rather, he won his spurs fighting against the remnants of the Orozquistas who, after their defeat at the hands of Huerta, scattered across the mountains from Chihuahua into Sonora.

As well as displaying an unusual—if amateur—military aptitude, Obregón also ran for mayor of his local town, Huatabampo, and won, which he did by appealing to diverse constituencies: friendly landlords, their 'gangs of peons', the local garrison, town officials (his brother was interim mayor), and the Mayo Indians, who were mobilized by their Indian 'governor'. This was a real election—not a top-down imposition, Porfirian-style—but it also involved some shrewd politicking, allied to a populist style (Obregón, for example, could speak Mayo to the Mayos). Again, this phenomenon pointed the way forward: not necessarily to a pristine liberal-democratic politics, as Madero had hoped, but at least to a politics that genuinely involved both 'mass publics' and a new kind of populist campaigning.

Populism was not Madero's forte. The political capital he had initially enjoyed—as the victor of 1911—was soon spent. He relied excessively on the army (as his erstwhile revolutionary allies charged), yet he seemed incapable—as his vocal critics on the Right complained—of restoring peace and order. His original political platform consisted of one big plank—electoral democracy—but the implementation of this key promise was vitiated by continued warfare, as well as the difficulties of installing democracy after more than thirty years of Porfirian authoritarianism. Conflict plus inertia were inimical to the creation of consensus, which was—and is?—the necessary basis of a functioning democracy. To put it differently: it was supremely difficult for Mexicans to institute, almost overnight, a new (democratic) system, when old-regime interests were hostile, and popular revolutionary forces sought radical policies of land and labour reform. This had nothing to do with some enduring Mexican psyche (the legacy of Hispanic colonialism or the sanguinary Aztecs). Democracy is best learned and tested over time, and Madero had very little time; it is also best learned and tested in societies which are not racked by class, ethnic, and regional tensions, as Mexico was in 1911–12. To that extent, Madero's failure was, if not inevitable, at least heavily 'over-determined'.

As opposition candidate and, now, incumbent president, Madero had never promised sweeping social reform. He was aware of social tensions, in both city and countryside, but he proposed that they should be mediated and resolved through the ballot box—a proposal which, in the conflictual circumstances of 1911–12, was naively optimistic. For Madero, solutions—to the agrarian problem or the demands of labour—would have to be legal and consensual, not the work of an arbitrary executive. Property rights had to be respected; at best, the state could distribute public land or revamp the—pitifully low—land tax in order to encourage redistribution. The question of land reform was debated in Congress (even if they remained beyond the political pale, the insurgent Zapatistas at least helped place the question on the national agenda); but no decisive action followed. Liberals like Madero also agreed that better education was essential, but education took time and money and, since the government's priority was survival, the expanded military took an increasing share of the budget (up from 20 per cent to 26 per cent of total spending), at a time when government revenue was, at best, static.

In one area, however, the government did innovate, since innovation made political sense and came cheap. The urban working class emerged from the 1910–11 Revolution with heightened hopes and better organization. Strikes came thick and fast (though with modest results); employers lamented the loss of discipline and the spread of subversive ideas; and workers, especially those in key sectors (ports, railways, textiles), forged opportunistic alliances with rising—often 'populist'—*políticos*. This represented less a dramatic U-turn than an acceleration of incipient trends evident in the late Porfiriato, when a few far-sighted politicians—such as Governor Dehesa of Veracruz—came to see organized labour less as a threat to be repressed, than a challenge to be met and, perhaps, an ally to be courted. Compared to the insurgent campesinos—often depicted as dark barbarians wielding bloody machetes—the urban workers, especially the literate artisans, seemed sober and civilized, members of a common urban culture, worthy of political redemption.

Amid the ideological ferment of the day, in which liberal, nationalist, socialist, and anarchist currents swirled, the left-wing Casa del Obrero Mundial ('House of the World Worker') was set up in Mexico City, chiefly by radical artisans who advocated socialist-cum-anarchist policies hostile to capital, foreign investment, and the Church. In response, Madero's government created a new Department of Labour, whose task was to counter radical appeals, to display the state's solicitude for working-class interests, and to monitor and mediate labour relations (in short, to deter strikes). Again, Madero fell before this initiative could achieve results, but it pointed the way forward: to a state–labour alliance which would underpin political stability and social reform.

# Chapter 4
# Counter-revolution and Constitutionalism (1913–1914)

## Enter the army

Madero fell: how and why? Popular protest, as I have suggested, could test and weaken the regime, driving it into the Judas-embrace of the army; but, as the defeat of Orozco showed, it could not topple the central government. Only the army could do that and, in February 1913, it did. Madero had built up the army, conferring increasing de facto power on its generals (notably Victoriano Huerta). Like Allende in Chile sixty years later, he thus mortgaged his regime to the military. The officer class—still overwhelmingly Porfiristas who hankered after the old regime—objected to Madero less because he was a radical reformist, which he wasn't, than because he was an ineffectual civilian—short of stature, with a squeaky voice and idiosyncratic beliefs, such as spiritism and homoeopathy. He required them to do his counter-insurgency dirty work (which they often relished), but he did so with much liberal hand-wringing and lamentation. The army believed they could do a better job under more congenial leadership: one of their own, unfettered by liberal misgivings, in the mould of old Don Porfirio. And there would no doubt be fat pay-offs and kickbacks along the way.

Arrested for subversion, Bernardo Reyes and Félix Díaz languished in gaol in Mexico City. (His advisers had urged Madero to have them swiftly executed; but, again, liberal scruples held him back.) In February 1910 they were sprung from gaol in order to head a military uprising in the capital. As the rebels marched on the National Palace—expecting the doors to be flung open by friendly forces—a fusillade of shots rang out and Reyes was killed. Díaz, the junior partner, took refuge in a military arsenal in central Mexico City and, for the following ten days (known as the Decena Trágica, the 'Ten Tragic Days') the capital, for the first time, experienced the horrors of civil war, as shells arced across downtown plazas and machine guns strafed the streets. The stand-off was resolved by means of treachery. Appointed commander of Madero's loyalist forces, Huerta contrived that they would be repulsed, with heavy losses, while he entered into clandestine negotiations with the rebel leaders, the US Ambassador, Henry Lane Wilson, offering his services as a sympathetic mediator. Finally, Huerta switched sides, arrested Madero, and had him surreptitiously killed, at dead of night. He then engineered a congressional farce, whereby he was appointed interim president. His allies—notably Félix Díaz—believed that interim meant interim; but Huerta had other ideas.

The coup of February 1913, involving both the overthrow and the killing of Madero, had decisive effects. Huerta and his allies, apart from promoting their own careers, hoped to return to the *belle époque* of the Porfiriato, for which they enjoyed the support of the old elite, the military, most foreign interests, and a significant section of the Catholic Church, whose celebration of the coup did not go unnoticed. In fact, far from turning the clock back, the coup set it running fast forward. That is to say, it resolved many of the contradictions which had vexed the Revolution since 1911 and ensured a renewed—now more prolonged and definitive—conflict between the forces of revolution and the forces of reaction.

By the time of his death Madero had lost most of his earlier popularity. But as a martyr to democracy, he became a potent symbol of resistance. Unlike the elites, the majority of the Mexican people (as we know from detailed American consular reports) opposed the coup; even if they could not immediately resist, they grudgingly consented, awaiting the right moment to turn sullen resentment into outright rebellion. Resistance was difficult because Huerta had the army on his side and his immediate policy was one of root-and-branch repression: 'peace, cost what it may' was his slogan. For the likes of Zapata, he told a British diplomat, the only solution was an 'eighteen-centavo rope' with which to hang him, as any common bandit deserved. A career soldier, whose—very successful—career had involved a series of counter-insurgency campaigns, culminating in his defeat of Orozco in 1912, Huerta had scant grasp of politics and saw the 'iron hand' as the only way to govern Mexico's wayward masses. Though he wanted to emulate Don Porfirio, he had none of the latter's political acumen; and he faced the challenge of mounting popular protest, which demanded political as well as military responses. The so-called 'psychology of military incompetence' has few better representatives in history than Victoriano Huerta.

Huerta boosted the military, replacing elected governors with hand-picked generals, while sidelining both cabinet and Congress. Congress was closed at bayonet-point in October; and Huerta's 'cabinet' consisted of a handful of cronies who often conducted business in the up market cantinas of Mexico City, where Huerta slaked his prodigious thirst for fine French brandy. Popular rebels like Zapata were under no illusion and fought on, their resolve stiffened by the sudden turn of events in the capital; after all, they knew Huerta at first hand as a brutal military commander in Morelos. The same was true of many minor rebels—like the Cedillos of San Luis—who saw no reason to surrender to a government which considered them troublesome bandits, worthy of the noose. One notable exception was Pascual Orozco who, completing his bizarre political odyssey, came out of the wilderness to ally with his old nemesis, Huerta. In the main, however, Huerta relied exclusively on the old Federal army and, in reaction, many of the components of the fragmented Maderista coalition now began to reassemble and reorganize. The Huerta coup thus brought fresh clarity to the political scene: the Revolution—in all its social and regional diversity—revived, and the old regime, betting the bank on the army, made a final but, as it turned out, disastrously counterproductive attempt to restore the Porfiriato by force of arms.

## The Revolution regroups

In this new situation, the big northern frontier states—Coahuila, Chihuahua, and Sonora—played a key role. They had contributed disproportionately to the Maderista rebellion in 1910–11. As a result, they had also experienced greater political renovation than states in central or, a fortiori, southern Mexico. New men had come to power, especially at the grassroots—Alvaro Obregón, newly elected mayor of Huatabampo, being a good example. A historic antipathy to the distant and capricious authority of Mexico City was now heightened by the fear that Huerta would snatch away their political gains. Huerta did nothing to allay that fear. In Chihuahua, reformist Governor González was deposed by the military and peremptorily murdered. Northern leaders took note: yielding to Huerta could be highly dangerous; perhaps valour was the better part of discretion.

That was the conclusion of Coahuila's governor, Venustiano Carranza, a crafty old *político* who had held office under Díaz and, rather unusually, backed Madero (who also came from Coahuila). As governor, Carranza had urged Madero—in vain—to beware of the burgeoning Federal Army. In response to the coup, Carranza prevaricated, bought time, then, in March 1913, repudiated the Huerta regime, calling for a restoration of constitutional rule; hence the generic label of his Revolution—Constitutionalism—and the narrowly political manifesto (the Plan of Guadalupe) which began it. Carranza had the support of a small state militia, but it was no match for the Federals so, styling himself 'First Chief of the Constitutionalist Revolution', Carranza made the long overland trek to the north-west, where the state government of Sonora had also rebelled, though more successfully.

The Sonoran revolt was a coordinated movement, involving the state administration and militia, capable of drawing on the state's rich resources (cattle and mining) to acquire arms from the US, albeit illegally and therefore expensively. Sonora enjoyed an additional advantage: it lay 1,000 miles from Mexico City and there was no direct railway link. By the time Huerta could dispatch troops to the north-west, the Sonoran revolution was up and running, an affirmation of regional autonomy and political representation in the face of military authoritarianism. The pioneer Sonoran rebels thus created a safe haven where Carranza and others could congregate; and they formed the key nucleus not only of the forces that would defeat Huerta, but also of the coalition which would eventually win the Revolution and create the revolutionary state of the 1920s, Alvaro Obregón and Plutarco Elías Calles foremost among them.

The final piece in the northern jigsaw was Chihuahua, the pioneer revolutionary state of 1910–11, which now reprised its role in opposition to Huerta. Here, the brutal Federal takeover had decapitated the state government, so an orderly Sonoran-style resistance was impossible. Instead, popular opposition to Huerta—which was extensive—was forged from the ground up, by local leaders, one of whom now shot to prominence: Francisco (Pancho) Villa who, along with Zapata, would become the great popular caudillo of the Revolution. (A hundred years later, Villa and Zapata are still the revolutionary leaders most recognized and revered in Mexico.)

Villa, born Doroteo Arango, came from a poor peasant family; as a teenager he fell on the wrong side of the law (versions vary, but a defence of family honour was probably involved); and he carved out a reputation as an intrepid bandit, rustler, and petty trader. With this experience under his belt, he provided useful service to the early Revolution in Chihuahua. Orozco's revolt and defection to Huerta removed the state's most famous popular rebel leader and Villa—who had only recently escaped from a Mexico City gaol—stepped into the breach.

He rapidly built a following among fellow-bandits and bushwhackers, cowboys, peasants, miners, railway workers, and middle-class activists who opposed Huerta and saw in Villa the kind of popular caudillo who could mount an effective armed opposition. Uneducated—indeed, illiterate until he had recently learned to read while in gaol—Villa was shrewd, audacious, and popular. His bandit past gave him an intimate knowledge of the centre-north, its people and places. He was motivated by a genuine urge to uplift the common people (he was particularly keen on providing basic education) and to punish the arrogant elites—notably the local Creel/Terrazas faction—who had profiteered from the Porfiriato and brought about Madero's overthrow and death. Villa felt a personal debt to the martyred president and many of Madero's family gravitated into the Villista camp. Villa's political vision may have been somewhat inchoate and unsophisticated; but he had no doubt about the righteousness of the Revolution and, as he rapidly mobilized forces in the north, he soon showed himself to be a bold and resourceful military commander.

While the continued Zapatista revolt in Morelos, now seconded by well-organized rebellions in the north, confronted Huerta with his biggest military challenge, resentment at the coup was apparent throughout Mexico and soon began to translate into armed opposition. As in 1910–11, rebellions tended to be localized, improvised, and initially poorly provisioned. But they were ubiquitous; and many of the later leaders of the revolutionary regime now made their names leading local forces against Huerta's army: the Cedillos in San Luis, Joaquín Amaro in Michoacán, the Gutiérrez brothers in Coahuila. Huerta thus faced two kinds of challenge: a potential advance by the burgeoning northern armies, soon capable of conventional campaigning; and a series of local insurrections, loosely allied to the northern Constitutionalists, many of them following the precedent of Zapatismo, by virtue of being peasant-based, agrarian, and committed, initially, to guerrilla warfare.

## Militarization

Huerta's response, again indicative of the 'psychology of military incompetence', was to boost the army and rely on repression. He broke with his erstwhile civilian allies—Félix Díaz fled into exile in fear of his life—and created a thoroughgoing military regime. Military commanders ran the states, extracting resources as they saw fit. Congress was ignored, closed down by force, and then reconvened as a Huertista talking shop. The press was censored and dissident journalists were gaoled, sometimes murdered. The Federal Army payroll soared: from 20,000 in 1910 to 250,000 in 1914. In part, this was fiction: padded payrolls put money into officers' pockets. But the cost still mounted, in terms of both blood and treasure. The military budget spiralled out of control; and, when the government's dwindling revenue could not meet rising current expenditure, Huerta printed money. Since the rebels had begun their own paper-money production, Mexico began to drown in a polychromatic tide of pretty banknotes. Inflation rose, starting a cycle that would reach hyperinflationary levels in a couple of years. Mexico's credit, carefully husbanded under Díaz, collapsed: Huerta defaulted on the national debt; and, for over a generation, Mexico was cut off from foreign loans.

This did not prevent Huerta from acquiring arms abroad—initially from the US, also from Europe and Japan—on a grand scale. For a year the Federals heavily outgunned their opponents, who lacked artillery, had inferior small arms, and were chronically short of ammunition. What the Federals lacked was committed manpower. The Huertista cause was deeply unpopular, so voluntary recruitment proved impossible. Appeals were made to the landed class, but Mexico's *hacendados* were no warrior aristocracy and—as

Luis Terrazas commented in Chihuahua—if guns were given to the peons, they might well be turned on the peons' masters.

The only alternative was forced recruitment, which had a long history in Mexico, but which elicited strenuous opposition, resistance, and evasion. In some cases, hitherto quiet regions—like the northern highlands of Puebla, where Indian communities lived on the margins of both state and market—were provoked to rebellion by the Federal recruiting sergeant. The press-gang (the *leva*) was also at work in the major cities, rounding up men and boys from the trams and the markets, seizing them as they emerged from bullrings and cinemas. Of course, such reluctant conscripts made poor soldiers: when they could they deserted (and by the spring of 1914 desertion was rife); and officers were leery of heading into open country with sullen armed conscripts at their backs. Though the Federal Army fought well, especially when it dug into fortified towns, its morale was always suspect; it readily surrendered the countryside to rebel forces; and, during 1914, its will to win collapsed in the face of successive defeats.

For the rebels to exploit Federal weakness and triumph, they had to make the difficult transition from guerrilla to conventional warfare—something they had not had time to do in 1910–11. The northern forces pioneered this transition; Zapata and others in central Mexico advanced more slowly down the path of professionalization, retaining a closer organic link with their local peasant communities, while the freewheeling northern armies undertook prodigious feats of recruitment, supply, and logistics. (The title of Obregón's meticulous autobiography says it all: *Ocho mil kilómetros en campaña*—'eight thousand kilometres on campaign'.)

## The role of the US

A key actor in this transition was the United States. Thus far, the role of the US in the Revolution was fairly marginal. American economic interests were part of the fabric of Mexican economic life, especially in the north, but that did not mean that resentment against those interests fuelled the Revolution. In fact, the evidence for this common assertion is thin. Some American interests were resented—for example, because they discriminated against Mexican workers, as they did at Cananea, or on the railways—but this was in no sense a major cause of the Revolution. Most revolutionary leaders—Madero, Villa, Carranza, Obregón—maintained pragmatic relations with American interests (which yielded valuable resources and revenue). In fact, rather greater hostility was shown by Huerta and the army; in part because of the army's ingrained anti-Americanism, but also because of evolving US policy towards Mexico.

Republican President Taft had maintained generally good relations with the Madero government; but his Ambassador in Mexico City, Henry Lane Wilson, increasingly—and vitriolically—denounced the embattled president, applauded his overthrow, and even helped smooth Huerta's Machiavellian path to power. (These were the days when ambassadors were important, not just decorative; and when, as in this case, they could pursue policies independently of their distant governments.) Huerta's coup coincided with the arrival of Woodrow Wilson in the White House, thus of a Democratic administration, critical of big business and dollar diplomacy and, eventually, committed to a liberal-interventionist foreign policy—first in Mexico, then in war-torn Europe. Indeed, Mexico provided the first major scenario for Wilson's 'new diplomacy'.

While cynical Europeans might view the ouster and killing of Madero as the usual Mexican way of doing things (which they viewed with equanimity, just as they hailed Huerta as the 'strong man' whom the wayward Mexicans needed), Wilson came to believe that Mexico was ripe for democracy, even social reform. Initially, he refrained from recognizing the new Huerta government; and he recalled Ambassador Wilson, preferring to rely on a series of trusted special emissaries who were sent to report on Mexico (which they did, often very unreliably). Through the summer of 1913 Huerta continued to import arms legally from the US, while the northern rebels had to rely on limited and expensive shipments of contraband weapons. This illegal trade made fortunes for US arms dealers, but it was also made possible by the strong sympathy for the Revolution evident in American border communities, especially their Mexican/Latino populations.

When Huerta forcibly closed Congress in October, Wilson sealed the border; and, four months later, he decided to allow the legal export of arms to the rebels—a crucial decision which enabled the northerners to equip major conventional forces that could take the war to the Federal Army. Wilson's decision, which cynical European observers deplored, was not—as the Europeans surmised—designed to prolong the war and facilitate an American takeover; rather, Wilson wanted to speed the victory of the Constitutionalists, end military tyranny, and help create a stable, representative polity south of the border. Indeed, his most egregious intervention, as ill-advised as it was counterproductive, was the seizure by American naval forces of the Atlantic port of Veracruz in April 1914: a ploy designed to cut off Huerta's arms supply and hasten his fall which, in fact, did neither, while it enabled Huerta to play the nationalist card (if to little effect), while seriously straining American relations with the rebels.

Flawed in its execution, Wilson's policy nevertheless made sense. While the name—'Constitutionalists'—no doubt appealed to Wilson's liberal academic sensibilities, the president was also aware of the social tensions underlying the Revolution and accepted the need for a land reform, not least because the Constitutionalists had effectively lobbied in Washington, gaining the ear of the president himself. And, while Wilson's grasp of events in Mexico was often naive and patchy, it was certainly better—that is, more sound and coherent—than that of his European counterparts, who, viewing things through racist and colonialist lenses, clung stubbornly to the belief that the Revolution was systematic banditry and that Huerta was Mexico's last best hope for a successful neo-Porfirian solution.

## The triumph of the Revolution

In spring 1914, with the US arms embargo lifted, the northern armies could acquire rifles, machine-guns, artillery, and ammunition sufficient to accelerate their advance on Mexico City. While Obregón led his—predominantly Sonoran—forces down the west coast, already displaying remarkable military flair, Pancho Villa's Division of the North, 15,000-strong and growing, equipped with troop trains (see Figure 3), artillery, and medical services, tightened its control on Chihuahua and advanced on the key north-central city of Torreón, in the heart of the Laguna cotton country. Here, in April, the rebels battled their way across the fields, canals, and hills north of the city, finally overcoming tenacious Federal resistance.

3. Revolutionary troop train, *c*.1914, by which time, especially in northern Mexico, guerrilla ('asymmetric') warfare had given way to major conventional campaigns, in which railways were key.

The victory opened the way to Mexico City and further broke Federal morale: subsequent battles at Zacatecas, San Pedro, and Orendaín, near Guadalajara, ended in Federal routs and heavy losses. At Zacatecas alone, 6,000 Federals—perhaps half the defending force—were reckoned to have been killed: a sober reminder for those who assert that Mexican-revolutionary battles were noisy and amateurish *fiestas de balas* ('carnivals of bullets') in which—compared to Europe in 1914–18—few actually died. Torreón made clear that Huerta's days were numbered, which was why the US occupation of Veracruz in the same month served no useful purpose.

It was now just a matter of time. The northern armies converged on Mexico City; Zapatista forces and their allies dominated an increasing area to the south of the capital; and a swathe of semi-autonomous rebels penned the Federals into their remaining beleaguered garrison towns. In August, as the Great War began, rebel forces approached Mexico City; Huerta resigned and took a ship to Europe, leaving an interim administration whose sole task was to negotiate the surrender of the nation's capital. This pattern—of rural and provincial armed forces converging on a fearful conservative capital—roughly resembles the pattern of the Chinese Revolution, but not the French (where Paris stood for Jacobin radicalism, when much of the countryside was hostile). While this comparison clearly subverts Samuel Huntington's—odd—notion of 'eastern' versus 'western' revolutions (the Mexican Revolution being, by Huntington's criteria, distinctly 'eastern'), it confirms Eric Wolf's thesis of a 'peasant war', which mobilized country people, under provincial and popular leadership, against the capital and the old regime interests headquartered there.

# Chapter 5
# The Revolution in power (1914–1920)

## Personnel and policy

The final defeat of Huerta and his army—thus, more consequentially, of the old regime which they fought to shore up—brought decisive changes. While the Madero revolt of 1910–11 had been halted in mid-course, the Constitutionalist revolution was a fight to the finish. 'A Revolution which compromises is a lost Revolution,' as Carranza pronounced; and he decreed that captured Federal Army officers should be summarily shot for treason, which they regularly were. The war polarized Mexican society and, by demanding heavy sacrifices, instilled an icy realpolitik into revolutionary practice: as winners, the rebel leaders of 1914 had no intention of emulating Madero's naive optimism. They would purge opponents and impose their will by force; in August 1914 Carranza closed the law courts and suspended all constitutional guarantees. This new radicalism—new, at least, in comparison to Madero's earlier magnanimity—had three dimensions: personnel, policy, and practice.

First, the 1913–14 revolution brought to power a clutch of new, young, mostly military leaders, who had fought their way to power—national, regional, and local—and who, for reasons of both idealism and ambition, intended to assert their authority. Most were in their thirties: in 1914 Zapata was 35, Villa 36, and

Obregón just 34 (Carranza, at 55, was of a different generation, which mattered). They came from the provinces, were rarely educated beyond basic schooling, and had close ties to their popular following (whose opinion Zapata, in particular, took very seriously). Many of them, like Obregón or Villa, cultivated an easy-going populist style, mixing with the common soldiers, sharing jokes, distributing handouts to the poor (such as cheap beef in Chihuahua), ostentatiously humiliating the rich and powerful (thus, Obregón issued brooms to the well-to-do of Mexico City and forced them to sweep the streets of the capital). And, without overly romanticizing the relationship, it is clear not only that these new politico-military leaders were qualitatively different from their Porfirian predecessors (being younger, browner, and more plebeian), but also that they wielded a different kind of authority, authority that was more broad, popular, and in some cases—Villa, Zapata, Obregón—charismatic.

Of course, enemies of the Revolution saw all this as mere demagogy and rabble-rousing (and there is no doubt that revolutionary populism coexisted with a good deal of self-seeking ambition and profiteering). But the Revolution was much more than that; and the creation of a new and deeper relationship between leaders and led, state and people, was an important consequence of the broad mobilization of these years. Total war helped forge a new 'social pact', as it would in post-1945 Europe.

Second, extensive fighting coupled with political polarization served to radicalize revolutionary goals, especially in socio-economic terms. Or, we could say, social reform now trumped political democratization—which, in the context of 1914, seemed a remote and risky objective: look what had happened to the naively democratic Madero. During 1913–14, land reform became a staple of rebel manifestos, espoused—probably opportunistically—even by the elderly and conservative Carranza. Villa, too, promised a *reparto de tierras* (land distribution), even though the demands of his massive military campaigns deterred immediate action, since the Villista government depended on hacienda production of cattle and cotton for revenue and any sudden radical *reparto* might have led to the rapid dissolution of the army, as soldiers scrambled to get their promised patrimony. However Zapata, and many lesser rebel leaders, notably in central Mexico, were not so inhibited. Their forces were less professional, more closely tied to the villages, hence a sweeping land reform was possible, even in the midst of armed revolt.

In Morelos, as Zapatista agrarianism grew more radical, the sugar plantations were carved up and local villages took possession of their fields and water. Similar processes, if less sweeping, affected other parts of Mexico: under the Cedillos in San Luis; or with the insurgent Yaqui Indians of Sonora—some of whom fought alongside Obregón, while others campaigned independently, and successfully, to recover control of their ancestral lands in the Yaqui River Valley. This de facto land reform was legitimized by laws and decrees from above, which laid down—in vague prospective terms—that haciendas could be stripped of their holdings in order to assuage peasant land hunger. Reform went beyond the matter of land distribution and also addressed the problem of debt-peonage, a key question as the northern rebels began to turn their attention to the benighted south, where peonage still flourished and the Revolution had made much less headway. In all these instances, revolutionary social reform had an obvious political dimension: it rewarded—and very likely swelled—the revolutionary rank-and-file, while punishing the landlord class who had, by and large, supported Huerta.

Hacienda peons were, by definition, landless labourers and, when it came to the working class, the revolutionaries again flaunted their social reformism, evident in a swathe of laws and decrees which established the minimum wage, protected workers' rights, and favoured trade union organization. While much of this, too, remained at the level of promise and prospectus, it was no mere froth: the workers—notably in the big textile factories east of

Mexico City—were autonomously organizing (one historian speaks of a 'revolution within the revolution'), taking advantage of the political upheaval to press their jittery bosses for wage rises and fringe benefits. Indeed, wage rises were essential at a time of mounting inflation.

While land and labour reform were hardly novelties—they had been evident since the early days of the Revolution—a new policy now became evident: revolutionary anticlericalism. This is a crucial but contentious subject, to be discussed in Chapter 6, dealing with the 1920s, when religious conflict reached its zenith. But its origins date to 1913–14. Madero had happily tolerated Catholic politicization, as we have seen; but his fall, and the subsequent hardening of political antagonisms, soon involved the Church, which was blamed by the rebels for aiding and abetting the Huerta regime. Of course, the Church was a large and diverse institution which, for all its authoritarian character, did not act as one. But certainly a good many clerics—particularly in the upper hierarchy—welcomed Huerta (as the potential bringer of peace and order) and some even preached accordingly. Parish priests were, in some cases, in cahoots with the landed class, thus bitterly opposed to agrarian protest and reform.

The Catholic National Party, in the main, collaborated with Huerta, even supplying several of his ministers in 1913 (for which it was hard to plead the excuse of *force majeure*). Thus the rebels, drawing upon an old reservoir of Mexican anticlericalism, blamed the Church—in general—for being antipopular and antinational. Sonoran leaders like Obregón and Calles—progressive, literate members of the provincial petty bourgeoisie—were particularly outspoken in their anticlericalism. In Mexico City Obregón arrested 180 priests and, effectively, held them to ransom, demanding a hefty pay-off which, he said, would be destined for poor relief; he also made much of the fact that a third of the detained priests were found to be suffering from venereal disease. In response, there were angry Catholic protests. And, across the country, revolutionaries of similarly Jacobin persuasion arrested (allegedly) subversive priests, closed convents, and turned parish churches into barracks, schools, even stables. In Monterrey the PLM veteran Antonio Villareal smashed the cathedral's old colonial statues and had the confessionals publicly burned.

Popular rebels, like Villa and Zapata, tended to be less committed anticlericals, although Villa hated—and persecuted—Spanish priests (more because they were Spanish than because they were priests). In response, the Church denounced revolutionary sacrilege, excommunicated the culprits, and actively lobbied against the Revolution in the US. The conflict ratcheted up, eventually culminating in the massive Catholic ('Cristero') revolt against the revolutionary state in the late 1920s.

Finally, revolutionary practice also became more radical in terms not just of policy but also of practice: radical ends required radical means. Unlike that of 1910–11, the civil war of 1913–14 was fought to the finish. Huerta fled, and along with him went a clutch of the old Porfirian elite, who flocked into exile in the US, Cuba, and Europe. Some would eventually return; a few even managed to rescue their family fortunes. But many never recovered and the revolutionaries, as they confiscated haciendas and took over the imposing town houses of the old elite in Mexico City, made it clear that they intended to supplant that elite, thus to reconfigure political—and to some degree socio-economic—power.

A key example was the Federal Army, the mainstay of the Huerta regime. Where Madero had maintained, conciliated, and bolstered the army, the victorious revolutionaries of 1914 simply abolished it. The conscript rank-and-file went home or joined the rebels; indeed, they had been deserting in droves well before the final debacle of summer 1914. The surviving officers either followed the Porfirian elite into exile or tried to carve out new careers in the chaos of Revolution. (A few—not many—managed to parlay their entry into the ranks of the Revolution: Villa seems to have been

more tolerant of this opportunistic entryism than Carranza.)
Meanwhile, even if the Constitutionalists nominally defended the
Constitution and the rule of law, they were, de facto, the military
masters of Mexico, who governed by decree, enacting reforms,
running the railways, confiscating goods, printing money, and
extracting taxes (not least from the remaining foreign enterprises,
notably the oil companies, then enjoying an export bonanza).
They confronted the Church and took a stern—though by no
means 'xenophobic'—line with foreign representatives: the British
Minister to Mexico, who had been a strenuous supporter of
Huerta, was promptly handed his passports.

## The revolutionary schism

Thus, by the summer of 1914, the Revolution—in all its topsy-turvy
variety—was victorious; but its achievements thus far were largely
destructive (eliminating the political old regime, weakening the
socio-economic order), while the constructive work of reform was
still incipient and inchoate. Two crucial and related issues now
occupied the political agenda: could the victorious rebels agree,
first, on a common programme and, second, on a common
government which would enact it? The subsequent story, spanning
the turn of 1914–15, revealed that the respective answers were:
yes, to some degree, and no. Because of the second answer, Mexico
descended into its third bout of civil war in five years—now, one
which pitted revolutionary against revolutionary, in a fratricidal
struggle (the 'war of the winners') whose logic remains a matter of
continued debate.

Hastily and chaotically assembled in order to fight Huerta, the
huge revolutionary coalition of 1913–14 was riven with internal
divisions—regional, factional, and ideological. Even before the
common task of defeating Huerta was over, major fissures began
to open up. These can be plotted at both the regional and national
levels. Regionally, Mexico had fallen under the control of caudillos
(warlords) and their forces who were jealous of their power: in

almost every state, potentially rival factions were warily eyeing each other—Maytorena's clique confronted that of Calles and his allies in Sonora; in Tlaxcala, Domingo Arenas competed with Máximo Rojas (even though both were popular leaders of peasant levies); in Chihuahua, where Villa was predominant, he faced dissent, notably from the powerful Herrera family of Parral. Such factional divisions are common in most revolutions; but in Mexico they were more acute, given both the size and heterogeneity of the country and the absence of a central party leadership (in Russia and China the respective Communist Parties battled for power, eventually successfully; in Mexico, no official revolutionary party was established until nearly twenty years after the outbreak of the Revolution, when the Partido Nacional Revolucionario was created in 1929). Thus, any potential revolutionary regime faced the problem of controlling and disciplining a host of ambitious regional warlords and their followers.

Nationally, we see the same problem writ large. The Revolution against Huerta involved, *grosso modo*, a loose coalition of the northern Constitutionalists, on the one hand, and the—less militarily powerful—Zapatistas and their allies in central Mexico. This fault line persisted: as Obregón's forces approached the capital, they were at pains, first, to get there before the Zapatistas and, second, to keep the Zapatistas—encamped only a few miles to the south—at arm's length. Negotiations between the Zapatistas and Constitutionalists proved tense and eventually broke down. But the northern Constitutionalist coalition was also falling apart. Here, the predictable fault line split Carranza and his Sonoran allies (notably Obregón) from Villa, the Division of the North, and its north-central base. Personal antipathies—and ambitions—played a part, perhaps also deeper politico-ideological differences (as I discuss shortly). Carranza was keen for Obregón to reach Mexico City before Villa and, allegedly, schemed to bring this about; as suspicions mounted, it was agreed that, once Huerta had been ousted, the revolutionaries would summon a national convention of the victors to thrash out Mexico's future. There would be no immediate elections, no swift return to constitutional rule; rather, the revolutionary military would debate and decide on the country's future.

The revolutionary convention duly met, representation being based (notionally) on the size of military contingents: one delegate for every 1,000 soldiers. First in Mexico City, then in the 'neutral' city of Aguascalientes to the north of the capital, the revolutionary convention spent most of October 1914 in speeches, arguments, horse-trading, and some drama—for example, when the Anarchist Díaz Soto y Gama, a representative of the Zapatistas, insulted the national flag and was nearly shot on the spot. The convention achieved some success in airing what were seen as the chief goals of the Revolution, including anticlericalism, labour reform, and land distribution. The Zapatista Plan of Ayala was thus formally accepted as a blueprint for the nation. In piecemeal fashion, the 'ideology of the Mexican Revolution'—an eclectic blend of social and political reform, coloured by nationalism and anticlericalism—began to jell. Again, we see the contrast with revolutionary Russia or China, where Marxism-Leninism became the canonical orthodoxy (albeit its interpretation was open to serious dispute), whereas in Mexico the revolutionary creed was cobbled together, over time and *ex post facto*, in the absence of canonical thinkers or texts.

When it came to the practical task of brokering a political settlement, however, the convention failed. The Zapatistas—chiefly smart-talking 'city boys', like Soto y Gama, sent as surrogate representatives by Zapata, who preferred to stay at home in Morelos—flaunted their radicalism and spurned compromise; the followers of Carranza and Villa, meanwhile, viewed each other with increasing suspicion. In the provinces, local caudillos watched events with trepidation, deciding how to jump if and when the time came. The time came when Villa effectively hijacked the convention, sending a large military force to occupy Aguascalientes. Factional divisions thus trumped efforts to

achieve revolutionary unity; though a rump 'Conventionist'
government survived, an increasingly irrelevant and itinerant
talking shop, it had no influence on the course of events, which
involved a fight to the finish between the two major factions: on
the one hand, Carranza, his loyal followers, and, above all,
Obregón and his proven Sonoran forces; on the other, Villa and
the Division of the North, loosely in alliance with the Zapatistas
(see Figure 4).

Local leaders had to react to this national schism, whether they
liked it or not; several switched sides back and forth, displaying,
not just cynical opportunism, but also genuine confusion and
uncertainty. Before long, skirmishing broke out.

Late in 1914 the Villistas and Zapatistas entered Mexico City,
forcing Obregón and his Carrancista forces to retreat to the east,

4. Meeting of the two great popular revolutionaries, northerner
Pancho Villa (left) and southerner Emiliano Zapata (right), outside
Mexico City, December 1914.

where the providential evacuation of Veracruz by the Americans gave the embattled Carranza government a temporarily safe bolthole. (It has also been argued that the Americans deliberately left a large arms cache in the port, in order to assist the Carrancista cause. This is unlikely: the Americans disliked the stiff-necked nationalist Carranza, finding Villa more congenial and compliant; and it seems probable that such matériel as they left was the result of cock-up rather than conspiracy—another episode in the long history of US forces mislaying military hardware on their extensive global travels.)

## The war of the winners: rationale

The scene was thus set for the final big bout of civil war (1914–15): one which, in contrast to the two previous bouts (1910–11, 1913–14), involved rival revolutionary forces, substantially similar in make-up and character. This raises a key question: what was at stake? And, by implication, a necessary counterfactual: how would Mexico have been different if, instead of the Carrancista victory which actually happened, Villa and his allies had won? There are three principal interpretations.

First, it could be argued that this was a simple battle for power between rival—yet similar—factions led by ambitious caudillos. In that sense, it did not matter much who won. While there is some truth to this interpretation (ambition and factional loyalty counted for a lot), it is by no means the whole truth. If more was at stake and the outcome did matter, the question arises: how did the factions differ—in terms of class, of ideology, of region, or of other criteria? And what did these differences imply regarding the military and political outcome? A standard interpretation, which also contains a modicum of truth, sees Villa—and his lukewarm ally Zapata—as popular leaders of peasant forces who offered a radical alternative, in contrast to Carranza and Obregón, who represented 'bourgeois' or 'petty-bourgeois' interests, thus a more moderate or conservative political option. It is certainly true that

Villa and Zapata were, individually, men of the people, from peasant stock, in which respect they differed from the ex-Porfirian *político* and landowner Carranza. (Obregón, a modest ranchero, was not so different. He also belonged to the same generation as Villa and Zapata, while Carranza was twenty years older.)

However, we must look beyond the background of a few prominent leaders. If we consider programmes, ideologies, and social support, the differences fade. The Zapatistas, it is true, were dogged agrarians, committed to land reform; but they were secondary allies of the Villistas, who were clearly the major players in the partnership. Yet the Villistas sponsored no sweeping land reform, and their official manifestos were no more radical than those of the Carrancistas—some of whom, like Salvador Alvarado, Plutarco Elías Calles, Francisco Múgica, and Lázaro Cárdenas, clearly stood on the left of the revolutionary spectrum. Indeed, when it came to labour reform, the Carrancistas had the edge: while both sides promised to improve the lot of urban workers, it was the Carrancistas who, early in 1915, struck a formal alliance with the radical Casa del Obrero Mundial ('House of the World Worker'), which led to the creation of the 'Red Battalions'—working-class detachments who fought, and fought with distinction, under Carrancista leadership.

The Carrancistas were also more strenuously anticlerical (so clerical/Catholic cities like Guadalajara clearly preferred Villa to Carranza), while the US, as well as the majority of foreign observers, came round to the view that Villa was the best bet, since he was a battle-hardened caudillo who seemed more amenable than the stubborn First Chief. So, the leftist American journalist Lincoln Steffens concluded, since Wall Street favoured Villa, Carranza deserved support.

If, in terms of personnel, the Carrancista camp included genuine radicals, there were also prominent Villistas who in no sense stood for popular power, still less socialism: José María Maytorena, member of a prominent Sonoran landed family; Manuel Peláez, a ranchero-rebel from the Huasteca, an ally of the Anglo-American oil companies; and several members of the well-to-do Madero family, who latched on to Villa because Carranza and his clique were hostile. Thus, if we take a broad view—beyond the top leadership of the rival factions—it becomes difficult to discern a clear class or ideological split. We find radicals, moderates, and conservatives, as well as bourgeois, petty-bourgeois, and popular leaders in both camps. In many cases, the Villista–Carrancista division appears to have been largely tactical: the two sides—in the state of Tlaxcala, for example—were substantially similar, in terms of social make-up and ideology. One final point is key: Villa's forces were, on paper, more formidable, seen as the likely winners of the impending conflict. Time-servers and opportunists—including a few ex-Federal officers—therefore went with Villa.

If clear class or ideological differences are hard to establish, does that mean that the conflict was meaningless, that a (counterfactual) Villista regime would have looked the same as the actual Carrancista/Obregonista one which emerged? Not necessarily. The Villista coalition was a loose, sprawling entity, embracing a wide range of social, ideological, and regional components, from Zapatistas on the Left to clerical, business, and ex-Federal Army interests on the Right. Furthermore, Villa's central control was, partly by choice, tenuous. The alliance with Zapata produced no effective joint military action. Self-styled Villistas in the centre and south waged their local wars under a political flag of convenience. The very size of the Villista coalition made it unwieldy and decentralized.

Furthermore, while Villa—like Zapata—had plenty of smart, educated advisers who urged national policies upon him, his inclination was to focus on Chihuahua and the centre-north, without producing a blueprint for national government. (Zapata, even more clearly, retreated into Morelos, happy to attend cockfights, father children, and preside over a radical local land reform.) The Carrancistas, in contrast, ran a tighter ship: their coalition, though smaller, was more centralized, with Carranza at the political helm and Obregón in control of the army (an army built around a strong Sonoran core). The Carrancistas rolled out a blueprint for centralized rule: they cut a deal with organized labour (hence, the Red Battalions); they confiscated church assets; they adopted a stern nationalist attitude towards the US (which contrasted with Villa's relaxed compliance); and they dispatched politico-military expeditions to the distant south-east—Yucatán, Oaxaca, Chiapas, states hitherto peripheral to the national revolution—in order to establish central control, to extract revenue, especially from Yucatán's profitable henequen industry, and to bring the benighted south—as they saw it, sometimes in racist terms—into the progressive revolutionary fold. Carrancista 'proconsuls', such as the Sonoran Salvador Alvarado, sent to govern Yucatán, were embodiments of the Carrancista/Sonora/ northern commitment to centralized national government, which would ram through radical—land, labour, and anticlerical—reforms, even in the face of local opposition.

Thus, irrespective of the relative radicalism of the warring factions, a key point of difference was the Carrancistas' commitment to centralized rule, which contrasted with the Villistas' relaxed tolerance of regional and sectoral heterogeneity. We can hypothesize that a counterfactual Villista regime, while it would certainly have accommodated some radical pockets (such as Zapatismo), would also have coexisted more happily with conservative and Catholic interests (in Jalisco, Oaxaca, the Huasteca), and would have been less likely to enact the kind of state-building and nationalist reforms which came about thanks to the Carrancista/Sonoran victory (see Chapter 6). The question in 1914–15 was not whether Mexico would go down a mythical road to radical socialism under Villa rather than (petty-?)bourgeois reformism under Carranza; it concerned, rather, the nature of the state and its relation to both civil society and foreign interests.

## The war of the winners: denouement

The outcome was determined in a series of major conventional battles fought in the Bajío region of centre-west Mexico in the spring and summer of 1915: Celaya, León, and Aguascalientes. Extensive fighting occurred elsewhere, notably at El Ebano, where the Carrancistas successfully defended their control of the oil region inland from Tampico, using trench-warfare tactics typical of the Western Front. But the key encounters in the Bajío involved the principal armies of Villa and Obregón—both experienced and well-organized revolutionary forces, possessed of stout morale, and numbering about 50,000 in total, the Villistas enjoying a distinct but not overwhelming advantage. Such major conventional armies needed constant supply by train (so, railway communications were key to the campaign as it unfolded); the Villistas enjoyed access to the US border, while the Carrancistas could import by sea to Veracruz. Though both sides faced occasional shortages, the outcome was not determined by the supply of munitions; nor did it reflect broad public opinion (which seems to have leaned to Villa) or even active social support (the Carrancistas fielded some 6,000 armed workers—the Red Battalions—who fought effectively; but their participation did not determine the outcome).

The result, rather, depended on Obregón's superior generalship, backed by a sound logistical system: his ability to supply and deploy his army as it advanced north into hostile Villista territory; and his military skill—perhaps genius—in the choice of terrain and tactics. Villa, who in 1913–14 had won his battles against armies of Federal conscripts, now faced a fellow-revolutionary who was a better general, leading confident, well-organized troops. At Celaya, Obregón stationed his forces among the canals and irrigation ditches outside the city, where his infantry, including machine-gunners, could cut down repeated Villista cavalry charges. Again at Trinidad/León—the key battle—and the final

Villista defeat and debacle at Aguascalientes, the Carrancistas resisted successive, impetuous attacks, before going on to the offensive and winning the day. Villa was advised to temper these rash and repetitive tactics, but he paid little heed. In war as in politics he had his own way of doing things—he was no plebeian puppet—but his swashbuckling approach, a sharp contrast to Obregón's cerebral generalship, proved disastrous when it came to conventional battles involving World War I military technology.

## The Carranza government: challenges and responses

By the end of the summer of 1915, Villa's army was broken and Villa himself was reduced to hit-and-run campaigns in the far north and north-west. Thanks to Obregón, Carranza had won; and his victory was franked by US diplomatic recognition in October. Preoccupied with events in Europe, the Wilson administration thus resolved—reluctantly—to endorse Carranza; a decision which Villa, hitherto tolerant of US interests, understandably saw as a perfidious betrayal. His scattered forces took reprisals against Americans, killing some seventeen at Santa Ysabel, then launching a violent, if futile, raid on the US border town of Columbus, New Mexico. The attack—the first foreign armed incursion on American soil since 1812—inevitably provoked a US military response (1916 was an election year, when Woodrow Wilson sought, and won, re-election).

Resisting red-blooded demands for a full-scale invasion, Wilson sent the so-called 'Punitive' Expedition into northern Mexico, its mission to pursue and eliminate Villa (see Figure 5). It failed. Villa, intimately familiar with the terrain, eluded pursuit; meanwhile, the expedition caused serious tensions with the new Carranza government, while endowing Villa, whose popularity was fast dwindling, with an aura of macho patriotism. But neither

5. Uncle Sam tries to discipline a wayward—and suitably swarthy and juvenile—Mexico, while Cuba, the Philippines, Nicaragua, and Panama, who are all the better (and the whiter) for having had the treatment, look on approvingly.

Wilson—aware that America's entry into the European War might be imminent—nor Carranza, governing a prostrate country, could countenance a full-scale war and, early in 1917, the expedition was withdrawn, its mission unfulfilled.

Villista raids and US intervention were not Carranza's only headaches. Zapata and his allies fought on, despite severe military repression. The south, chafing under the imposed 'proconsular' rule of northerners, remained restive and, under the leadership of local elites, the state of Oaxaca briefly seceded from the Federation. More broadly, conservative interests—landlords, ex-Federal officers, provincial elites, and foreign business—lent support to Don Porfirio's nephew, Félix Díaz (last heard of fleeing from the wrath of Huerta in 1913), who became the figurehead of a swathe of loosely counter-revolutionary (so-called 'Felicista') forces, chiefly in the south. These rebel forces, combined with a plague of mercenary banditry, severely compromised the regime's control of the country.

Apart from such armed challenges, Carranza headed the bankrupt government of a ravaged economy and a war-weary people. The flood of paper money produced hyperinflation, with all its attendant social consequences: a minority with access to hard currency (via exports) prospered, while the majority had to contend with depreciating paper and, eventually, a barter economy. Rich families, already threatened by land and labour reform, saw their fortunes evaporate, their property being seized or snapped up by parvenus with access to gold, dollars, or political power. The geographical mobility provoked by the Revolution—extensive campaigning, migration, and the flight of refugees to cities like the capital—was complemented by enhanced social mobility, the product not just of political renovation, but also socio-economic upheaval.

The labour movement, decisively boosted by the Revolution, now fought defensive battles to maintain falling living standards; the Casa's pact with Carranza soon came under strain, the Red Battalions were disbanded, and, when a general strike was called in Mexico City in August 1916, the government broke it by force. Meanwhile, the economy reached its nadir, a year or two after the fighting had peaked. The railways, still under military control, were in a parlous state and the banks' assets had been seized by a desperate government. Some export sectors—such as oil and henequen—remained buoyant, helped by wartime demand, but staple production slumped and dearth was widespread; 1917, historically celebrated as the year of the new Constitution, was known at the time as the 'year of hunger'. Armed conflict, material hardship, and spatial mobility also fostered disease, typically typhus—the classic disease of warfare—and, in 1918, the Spanish influenza pandemic, which, striking a war-weary and malnourished population, killed perhaps a quarter of a million Mexicans (this in addition to half a million victims of revolutionary warfare). Oral accounts of the Revolution remind us that, for many contemporaries, this was a time, not of joyful political advance, but rather of desperate struggle for subsistence.

Collective war-weariness helped the fragile regime survive. Rebels and bandits might defy the state, but they could not overthrow it. Meanwhile, Carranza and his allies struggled to survive and to forge a new revolutionary legitimacy amid the ashes of the old regime. We know, with hindsight, that they succeeded—eventually, quite decisively—but at the time this could not be foreseen. The infant Carrancista regime operated on two levels, displaying something of a schizoid character which would endure for decades in Mexican politics. Informally, the 'Constitutionalists' relied heavily on military force and repression; they controlled the press, as best they could, and, in the noisy nursery of infant political parties (the single official revolutionary party did not emerge until 1929), they promoted their own people and marginalized their enemies—including revolutionaries who had backed the wrong horse in 1914. Graft and corruption were common, facilitated by state control, or regulation, of large swathes of the economy: banks, railways, and some productive assets, such as the henequen of Yucatán or the booming oil industry, which was subjected to tighter control and heavier taxation. Madero's old dream of consensual liberal democracy was never realized. At the same time, however, Mexico's new leaders needed to garner popular support, to live up to—or, at least, not systematically traduce—their rhetorical claims to social reform and popular emancipation.

## The 1917 Constitution

The creation of a new Constitution was therefore a key goal, which would legitimize Carranza's administration, while setting out the Revolution's social-reformist stall. The condition of the country hardly allowed fair and free elections; furthermore, Mexico's new masters were determined to ensure that they controlled the Constitution-building process. Political enemies—Villistas and Zapatistas, as well as old Porfiristas—were proscribed and the Church, increasingly aggrieved by Carrancista anticlericalism, played no part. The *constituyentes* (elected representatives) who gathered at Querétaro in late 1916 were, therefore, Carrancistas to a man (and they were all men). However, the Carrancistas themselves were not of one mind. Carranza himself sought a rapid return to constitutional rule, envisaging a new charter that would roughly replicate that of 1857 (moderate, liberal, democratic, mildly anticlerical, with a smidgen of social reform thrown in).

But Carranza was out of step with popular demands and even with his own more radical allies, such as Obregón. The moderate draft which the First Chief and his chosen ideologues presented was mauled, amended, and substantially radicalized. The resulting Constitution of 1917 retained the political architecture of 1857 (a liberal-democratic federal and presidential polity), but acquired radical provisions debarring the Church from politics and primary education, while providing generous provisions for workers (Article 123: the 'Magna Carta of Mexican labour') and, most significantly of all, declaring, in Article 27, the 'social function of property', which gave the state the power to override private property rights in order to restrict/regulate foreign investment and enact sweeping land reform. Oddly, amid the long and loquacious debates held at Querétaro, Articles 123 and 27—the social provisions which made the Constitution one of the most radical of its time—were nodded through in haste, while the anticlerical measures provoked fierce debate—roughly, between moderate liberals and radical *comecuras* ('priest-eaters'), who had come to regard the Catholic Church as the Revolution's greatest enemy.

Carranza, though hardly enamoured of the radical document which emerged, at least had his Constitution and could thus be elected constitutional president, in an anodyne and closely controlled poll. At the same time, a new Congress, embodying the diverse currents of (Carrancista) opinion was elected, soon showing itself more than ready to defy the president's shaky authority. But, for all the radical rhetoric of Querétaro, reforms were slow in coming. While there had been an extensive de facto land reform during the years of armed upheaval, Carranza was reluctant to validate such measures (especially where they were the work of Zapatistas and other enemies) and, during his short presidency (1917–20), he stalled on agrarian reform. Indeed, in some cases he sought to restore land to erstwhile property-owners. But he could not halt the agrarian movement, which now began to adjust to the new dispensation, as armed revolt gave way to semi-legal politicking. The labour movement, too, saw few immediate benefits; but plenty of Carrancistas (among them Obregón and Calles) were fully aware that the unions were promising political allies who should be cultivated rather than repressed.

Fortunately for Carranza, the economy was now fast recovering, helped by wartime demand for Mexican oil, minerals, and henequen. After the disaster of 1917, harvests picked up, as well as consumer demand. By 1920, the economy had recovered its prerevolutionary level, affording a solid platform for the next administration. The clear consensus was that Obregón, the great Napoleonic victor of the Revolution, would head that administration. Carranza, again, showed himself to be out of touch. He attempted to impose his preferred, but unpopular, civilian candidate, provoking widespread military opposition. Carranza fled the capital and, en route to Veracruz, was slain—or, perhaps, committed suicide. Obregón was elected president and inaugurated what would be known as the 'Sonoran dynasty', a regime which carried the stamp of its north-western origins. The last violent change of government in the long revolutionary cycle had happened; thereafter, though political conflict continued, the state would never again suffer armed overthrow. The Revolution was here to stay.

# Chapter 6
# The institutional Revolution: The Sonoran dynasty (1920–1934)

## A politico-economic overview

During the decade of armed revolution, events—revolts, coups, battles—came thick and fast; since they were both cumulative and consequential, they demand, and have received, narrative treatment. After 1920, as political stability was painfully achieved, it becomes possible to adopt a more thematic and structural approach, focusing on the main features of the new revolutionary regime as it evolved. However, things still happened: serious military revolts and a bitter war between Church and State in the 1920s; then, the external shock of the Great Depression of the early 1930, which had a powerful impact on the course of the now institutionalized Revolution. This chapter will therefore focus on the evolution of the Revolution—the Revolution in power—during the 1920s, then Chapter 7 will examine how the Depression produced a lurch to the left and the last great reformist administration of the revolutionary period, that of President Lázaro Cárdenas (1934–40).

The overthrow of Carranza in 1920 was quick and relatively bloodless. Carranza died and many of his closest supporters escaped into exile. But the fundamentals of the regime remained much the same: in effect, the rebellion clarified the situation by allocating power to those who had won the Revolution—the

Sonoran leaders, their allies, both military and civilian, and their project of nationalism and socio-political reform. Obregón, the most powerful of those leaders, served as president in 1920–4, his principal achievements being to consolidate the regime and confound its enemies, both at home and abroad; he was succeeded by his fellow-Sonoran Calles (1924–8)—a more cerebral *político*, lacking Obregón's gladhanding charm (and military prestige), but driven by a ruthless commitment to building national power while enacting socio-political reform (as the Church found, to its cost).

When Obregón was re-elected in 1928, it seemed as if the Sonorans had established an alternating dyarchy (which avoided the immediate re-election of an outgoing president, as the Revolution had demanded and the new Constitution required, but allowed non-sequential re-election). But a Catholic militant, aggrieved by the regime's anticlericalism, then assassinated the president-elect. Since Calles, not Obregón, was the chief *comecuras* of the regime, the assassin chose the wrong victim; but we cannot, perhaps, expect political assassins to display discerning rationality. Amid the succession crisis which ensued, Calles displayed his political acumen: he declined to prolong his mandate (declaring, somewhat disingenuously, that it was now time for institutions rather than great men to rule the destinies of Mexico); he arranged for an interim presidency followed by a fresh election; and, most important, he set up a new, official, revolutionary party (the PNR: Partido Nacional Revolucionario), which absorbed into its great bulk most of the many hundred pro-regime parties which had proliferated throughout the 1920s. Initially a loose umbrella organization, the PNR gradually established itself as a hegemonic force, controlling most political offices, imposing central discipline on Mexico's fractious political class, and creating a civilian counterweight to the over-mighty military. Mexico was not a one-party state (weak rivals still existed); and, we should recall, the official party was born nearly two decades after the Revolution had begun. Unlike, for example, the Communist Party of the Soviet Union, it was the product, not the progenitor, of the armed revolution.

Though no longer president, Calles dominated politics for the next six years (1928–34), his role—that of 'jefe máximo' ('chief boss')—giving the period its title, the 'maximato', which came to an end with the presidency of Cárdenas (1934–40) and Calles's disgrace and exile. These were also years of economic upheaval, as the Great Depression hit Mexico (to be discussed in Chapter 7). Thus, in political terms, the years 1920–34 can be loosely called those of the Sonoran dynasty, years of political consolidation and reform which laid down the enduring foundations of the revolutionary regime.

Economic trends helped. By the early 1920s the economy had recovered from the ravages of the Revolution; though 1921 saw the peak of Mexico's (first) oil boom, coinciding with worldwide recession, a swift recovery followed; and, until 1926, the economy performed well. Exports—the same exports as in the days of Díaz—were buoyant, and, in part thanks to the incipient social reform of the period (land and labour reform), the domestic market expanded, to the advantage of manufacturing. Though oil went into gradual decline, foreign, chiefly American, investment in other sectors, including mining and manufacturing, increased. Revolutionary nationalism (of which more anon) did not mean autarky or xenophobia.

With economic growth, government income rose, enabling, in particular, the Calles administration to espouse more ambitious policies of educational provision, road-building, and irrigation. The state did not balloon, but it gradually grew, achieving greater engagement with civil society. Solid government finances also encouraged Calles to adopt more radical policies, especially in his confrontation with the Church after 1926. However, the ensuing conflict weakened the economy and strained government finances; at the same time, global trends (basically, falling demand for and prices of primary products) hurt the Mexican economy, which, during 1927–9, lost its dynamism. The 1929–30 Depression thus hit a flatlining economy and Calles, as he mutated from constitutional president to informal *jefe máximo*, moved to the Right, espousing orthodox, book-balancing financial policies (which were a mistake) and reining in what he now saw as dangerously radical measures in the fields of land and labour reform.

Against this backdrop, the Sonoran dynasty of the 'long' 1920s (1920–34) set about achieving political stability and ensuring the survival of the revolutionary regime. This process—ultimately successful—can be schematically analysed under six headings, each referring to a dimension of Mexican politics where the state faced serious challenges, as well as potential opportunities: the military; the peasantry; organized labour; the middle class; the Church; and the United States.

## Praetorian politics

The armed revolution left a legacy of a bloated army, a swollen military budget, and an excess population of politically ambitious officers (the Sonorans themselves being exemplary). The disgruntled army had easily ousted Carranza; and a massive military revolt, similarly triggered by the impending presidential succession, occurred in 1923–4, when Obregón tapped Calles as his successor, thus alienating a large swathe of the army. The ensuing ('de la Huerta') revolt was defeated, in part because the US lent its support to the incumbent government, but it was a close run thing. Lesser military revolts, again prompted by the vexed question of the presidential succession, occurred in 1927 and 1929. These, however, were more easily suppressed: thus it became clear that the central government was increasingly capable of resisting such challenges and dissident generals came to see the folly of rebellion.

Of course, the revolts themselves removed a large number of dissidents—in Darwinian fashion, the revolutionary military culled its own over populated ranks—and, at the same time, the surviving generals became older, fatter, and richer, thus less disposed to take to the hills, risking both life and livelihood.

Indeed, Obregón made a practice of buying off dissidents with lavish perks and hand-outs ('no Mexican general can resist a cannonade of 50,000 pesos' was his characteristically wry comment), while Calles, if less open-handed and less sympathetic to the military caste, ensured that loyal commanders were well rewarded with political posts and business opportunities. Obregón and Calles themselves acquired extensive business interests, as did many of their close allies. The *embourgeoisement* of the revolutionary military became a stock theme not just of political comment but also of mainstream literature.

At the same time, the regime set about slimming and professionalizing the army. The military share of the national budget fell from 53 per cent in 1921 to 30 per cent in 1926 and, after an upward tick in 1926–9 when spending jumped to 37 per cent because of the Cristero War (discussed later), it fell consistently through the 1930s, reaching just 16 per cent in 1939. Though the top generals—Obregón, Calles, Cárdenas, Amaro, Cedillo, Almazán—remained the political kingpins, civilian *políticos* expanded their role, especially in ministries—such as Finance and Foreign Relations—which required greater expertise. The revolutionary regime thus acquired a technocratic dimension (exemplified by men like Alberto Pani and Manuel Gómez Morín) alongside its military/populist bloc.

Joaquín Amaro, a rough-hewn mestizo of poor rural background, rose to become Minister of War; he ruthlessly pruned and professionalized the military, introducing new equipment, while tipping the balance of armed force in favour of the central government and against the pretensions of provincial caudillos. The latter came to see the wisdom of collaborating with—and not resisting—the growing power of the 'centre'. Those who failed to learn that lesson came to grief: for example, Adalberto Tejeda, the ambitious radical boss of Veracruz, who built a powerful regional political machine but was prised from power in 1935; and Saturnino Cedillo, revolutionary veteran and politico-military cacique of the state of San Luis Potosí, whose quixotic 1939 revolt was easily snuffed out.

## Populist politics: peasants and land reform

Thus, the Sonoran dynasty, its power initially premised on military accomplishment, successfully disciplined its own and achieved a necessary measure of demilitarization. To do this, it needed countervailing allies, in particular, the peasantry and organized labour. Both groups had played important, if contrasting, roles in the armed revolution: the majority peasantry had provided the rebel rank-and-file and, even as the fighting ebbed, they retained considerable leverage (not least because they retained their weapons and local capacity for resistance); while the minority labour movement, strategically located in major cities and key sectors like oil, mining, textiles, and the railways, took advantage of the Revolution to organize and to strike deals with rising caudillos (hence, Obregón's pact with the Casa which created the Red Battalions). The peasantry and the working class represented newly mobilized forces, capable of deploying their numbers both politically (for example, in elections or mass demonstrations) and militarily (indeed, the Sonoran state successfully recruited popular levies to resist the mutinous army in 1923–4, while agrarian paramilitaries were deployed against Catholic rebels in 1926–9). By such means both groups could advance their claims: to land distribution, in the case of the peasantry, and to labour reform—including the protection and advancement of the infant trade unions—in the case of labour.

The revolutionary state thus needed to retain popular support, if only to survive, while there were certainly revolutionary leaders, like Cárdenas, Múgica, and Tejeda, who felt a genuine commitment to social reform, as the Revolution had promised. Whether idealism or realpolitik determined the outcome (and, often, it is impossible to plumb the depths of political motivation and to distinguish the two), the result was a reformist thrust—often corrupt, demagogic, and violent, as revisionist scholarship stresses, but also novel, effective, and, within the broad panorama of Latin America in this period, unusually radical. We can also confidently conclude that, without the Revolution (that is, if Díaz or Reyes or Huerta had ruled in place of Obregón, Calles, and Cárdenas), these reforms would not have happened. The Revolution made a real difference.

Peasant mobilization embodied both local/regional and national forms. The latter—the Partido Nacional Agrarista (the National Agrarian Party)—had a voice in Congress where, under the leadership of the old Zapatista firebrand Soto y Gama, it claimed to speak for the peasantry. Its bark was worse than its bite; peasant mobilization was more effective at the local and regional (state) level. A key case was the state of Morelos, home of the Zapatistas. Zapata himself had been treacherously slain in 1919, but his movement lived on (some even denied that their old leader was really dead) and, under pragmatic leadership, the Zapatistas cut a deal with Obregón in 1920, as he assumed the presidency. They would support him (though not lay down their arms) and he would concede them a substantial measure of power and reform in Morelos.

This was of a piece with Obregón's strategy in 1920, when he cut deals right and left, in order to consolidate his power; in Chiapas, in the deep south, for example, he similarly delegated power to the so-called *mapaches* ('badgers')—conservative militias, recruited by local landlords, who had acquired their name by foraging in the open country. However, in states, notably in central Mexico, where the insurgent peasantry were an armed presence, the ensuing deals resulted in a measure of land reform, even peasant 'empowerment'. Thus, while the *reparto* (land distribution) of the 1920s was, in national terms, halting and patchy, it had a real impact in Morelos, where 69 per cent of cultivated land was transferred to peasants in the form of 'ejidos', that is, communal land grants vested in the community. This meant that, in Morelos at least, the dominance of the great estates was liquidated: a posthumous tribute to Zapata's struggle. Elsewhere in central Mexico, the proportion was less, but still significant: 22 per cent in Puebla, 20 per cent in Tlaxcala. The north and deep south were, in general, less affected.

The early *reparto* of the 1920s thus roughly reflected the strength of peasant insurgency in the previous decade. The ejido was a reward for services rendered to the Revolution; it was also a guarantee against future rebellion and a means to attach the peasantry to the paternalist revolutionary state. The nature of the ejido facilitated attachment: the grant was to the community, not to individuals; and it conferred usufruct, not ownership. Thereby, it was argued (quite sensibly), land grants could not be bought and sold, to the advantage of rich landlords; but the conditionality of the ejido made it an effective tool of state clientelism.

Peasants wanted—and had often fought for—land, hence they welcomed ejidal grants (for which, again, they had often struggled long and hard, litigating, lobbying, and petitioning). Ejidos frequently came with new rural schools, which were also generally welcome. But the conditionality of ejidal grants made their recipients clients of the state, which they did not necessarily wish to be. Many, it seems likely, would have preferred outright freehold possession. (The notion of deep peasant attachment to 'communal' forms of agriculture is often asserted, but also often exaggerated.) In some cases, such as Namiquipa, Chihuahua, a community of tough frontier people in the far north, the ejido was repudiated as an unwarranted intrusion into local affairs on the part of the central state. Such a reaction was not typical and, by and large, ejidos—even if they provided usufruct rather than ownership—were welcome. But they laid the basis for an extensive and enduring network of rural clientelism, with the agrarian cacique (local boss) acting as the key intermediary between the mobilized peasantry and the state. Again, conditionality enhanced the power of caciques, who could use dispossession, even expulsion, as political weapons.

Two other features of revolutionary agrarianism were crucial. During the 1920s, as the central state gradually consolidated, agrarian mobilization was often promoted by local or regional leaders: some, who had risen from the ranks of the peasantry (including the ranchero class), such as Cedillo in San Luis or Primo Tapia in Michoacan; some who achieved power, for example as governors, and looked to build rural clienteles on the basis of land reform (for example, Tejeda in Veracruz, Cárdenas in Michoacan, Portes Gil in Tamapulipas, and Felipe Carrillo Puerto in Yucatán). Again, motives were mixed: Portes Gil was an exemplary fixer who practised a form of pragmatic populism (distributing land and forging his own regional 'socialist' party in the process); Tejeda and Cárdenas did much the same, but in more radical and—perhaps—more idealistic fashion. Carrillo Puerto—a tall, green-eyed, middle-class journalist (see Figure 6)—rallied Maya peasants to his cause in Yucatán, sponsoring a brief, radical reform before he was overthrown and killed by the plantocracy in 1924.

Again, we see a complicated political jigsaw, involving contrasting patterns of radical reform, moderate reform, and outright reaction. As recent research confirms, the impact of the Revolution demands regional and local differentiation; national generalizations are risky.

We also see continued violence, much of it occurring out in the provinces, below the national radar. Carrillo Puerto was ousted and slain; Primo Tapia, the charismatic peasant leader from Naranja, Michoacan, was brutally done to death by thugs in the pay of local landlords. But, compared to the 'top-down' violence of the Porfirian old regime, agrarian conflict in the 1920s was a two-way street. Agrarian reformers like Tapia and Carrillo Puerto fell victim to what could be called 'counter-revolutionary' landlord violence; but landlords and their minions were now also casualties of continued agrarian confrontation. In Puebla, the histrionic American widow Rosalie Evans defended her hacienda against the

**6. Felipe Carrillo Puerto, the radical Governor of Yucatán, with Maya peasants, women to the fore; a champion of radical reform, Carrillo Puerto was, soon after, overthrown and killed by forces allied with the powerful Yucatán planter class.**

assaults—legal, political, and armed—of local agraristas led by Manuel Montes ('bandits' and 'Bolsheviks', as she called them, led by 'an arch-devil', a short, stocky Indian peasant, with 'the cruellest eyes, like a viper poised to strike...'). As she patrolled the perimeter of her embattled estate on horseback, accompanied by a pack of fearsome dogs, she saw herself as a champion of civilization against Indian barbarism and Bolshevism, until she was cut down by a sniper's bullet in 1924.

The Rosalie Evans story was unusual because of its international notoriety (most of the landlord-victims of land reform were Mexican, a few were Spanish); but it encapsulated several key features of 1920s agrarian conflict. Landlords now faced an unprecedented challenge from newly mobilized peasants (some considered 'Indians') and lamented the downfall of the old regime, as the alleged peace and prosperity of the Porfiriato gave way to demagogy and insurgence. Peasants saw their opportunities and, often at great cost, mobilized to claim land and a measure of local political power. Regional political bosses struck alliances (both for and against land reform), while the central government, itself torn between pro- and anti-agrarista factions, had to allow a measure of land distribution without, it was hoped, undermining the economy, alienating foreign confidence, or provoking a conservative backlash.

By the time of the Maximato (1928–34), as the Depression struck, the Mexican land reform stood at a crossroads. Calles, a northerner who had never warmly embraced *agrarismo*, was shifting to the Right, favouring financial conservatism and retrenchment. The ejido, he declared, had failed to foster a prosperous and productive farmer class. The *reparto* should be wound up. Some *políticos*—collectively called the 'veterans'—agreed and, indeed, the aggregate figures of land distribution began to tumble after 1929. However, strong agrarian lobbies, both national and local, argued that the reform had been too moderate and piecemeal. The Depression, followed by the rise to power of Lázaro Cárdenas, ensured that land distribution would rapidly revive after 1934, involving a frontal assault on the surviving, but weakened, hacienda system.

## Populist politics: organized labour

The peasantry, broadly defined to include peons (estate workers), represented a good two-thirds of the Mexican population (perhaps 10 million, including families); urban workers were a minority (approximately 2–3 million, including both artisans and proletarians); and organized labour—those who had (recently) joined unions—were a minority within that minority (a few hundred thousand: perhaps 10 per cent of urban workers, concentrated in the cities). But organized labour possessed leverage beyond their numbers: first, because they were located in key cities and sectors, where their numerical strength was concentrated (for example, in the textile towns of Veracruz and the oil camps of the Gulf coast; on the railways and in the mining centres of the north); and, second, because they seemed worthy allies of progressive *políticos*, with whom they shared a literate, newspaper-reading culture, tinged with anticlericalism, which set them apart from the supposedly backward and superstitious campesinos of the countryside. It made political sense to appeal to urban workers; and it was risky to leave them prey to more radical, subversive organizations, like the anarchistic Casa del Obrero Mundial or, after 1919, the nascent Mexican Communist Party.

Obregón—and other far-sighted revolutionary leaders—therefore made a pitch for working-class support, in return for which, even in the heat of the armed revolution, they offered practical benefits: wage hikes and other benefits, support for *sindicatos* (trade unions), material provision (buildings, printing presses), and political office for aspiring working-class activists. In 1918, as the armed revolution drew to a bitter conclusion, a working-class assembly, convened with official support at the northern city of Saltillo, set up a national labour confederation, the CROM (Confederación Regional Obrera Mexicana: The Mexican Regional Workers Confederation; the 'Regional' label signalled its anarchistic leanings). The leaders, notably Luis Morones, emerged out of radical, in many cases, anarchist, working-class circles, particularly in Mexico City; but, as the origins of the CROM suggested, they had decided to drop the more radical anti-state rejectionism of Anarchism in order to collaborate, conditionally, with the infant revolutionary state. Carranza, never a friend of organized labour, was lukewarm; but his heir-apparent, Obregón, who had already established his labourist credentials, struck a deal with the CROM (one of the many political deals which he made in his successful bid for the presidency) and, in return for the CROM's support, he endorsed labour reform and gave the CROM privileged access to state power.

His successor, Calles, whose base in the army was weaker, relied even more heavily on Morones and labour. Thanks to state patronage, the CROM's numbers grew from 7,000 in 1918 to over 2 million by 1927. These were paper numbers, inflated for effect.

But there was no doubt that the CROM enjoyed a dominant position in the burgeoning labour movement, dwarfing its Catholic and radical leftist rivals; only a few powerful independent unions (such as the railway workers) resisted the CROM's embrace, along with a handful of 'yellow-dog' (company) unions, promoted by business interests, for example in Monterrey. The CROM's influence derived partly from its role in labour arbitration procedures which, as a result of Article 123 of the new Constitution, afforded recognized—usually CROMista—unions a role, alongside business and the state, in resolving labour disputes (which, employers lamented, were all too common, indicating the demagogy and indiscipline which the Revolution had unleashed).

Strikes tended to decline through the 1920s, as the framework of corporatist mediation took hold; but this did not mean (as many have asserted) that the CROM served simply to control and deradicalize labour. In some sectors the CROM was a genuine, if also corrupt, vehicle of working-class advancement (the Teamsters of the United States may offer a rough parallel). In the textile industry, where the CROM was strong, real wages rose significantly during the decade, and bosses complained of the incessant demands of the workers: not just for increased pay and shorter hours, but also for better conditions, accident compensation, sick pay, and an end to the employment of women and children. (Mexican unions may have been progressive, but they overwhelmingly represented men and shared the prevailing macho culture of the time.) Compared to the plight of labour in other Latin American countries—Brazil would be a striking contrast, for example—Mexico's unions enjoyed a relatively privileged position—again, an indicator of the broadly progressive impact of the Revolution on Mexican society.

The CROM's power depended crucially on political access. It created an affiliated party—the Partido Laborista (PL, its name borrowed, it was said, from its British counterpart)—and by 1927 the PL provided 40 of 272 congressional deputies and 12 of 58 senators. This was a formidable bloc, centrally controlled; thus, the PL enjoyed greater leverage than its peasant counterpart (the PNA) and PL/CROMista leaders rose to high office. Morones became Minister of Communications and Public Works in Calles's cabinet, in which capacity he served the interests of the state, the CROM, the PL, and, perhaps most faithfully of all, Luis Morones himself. Like other revolutionary parvenus, Morones acquired fine town houses, Cadillacs, and diamond rings, which he flaunted on his pudgy fingers (to his critics he was the 'pig of the Revolution' and CROM stood for 'como robó oro Morones': 'how Morones stole the gold').

But—again consider trade union machines elsewhere—a measure of graft and enrichment did not prevent Morones from benefiting his members—who, ultimately, were the basis of his power—and, perhaps, giving them the psychological satisfaction of seeing one of their own sitting in the back seat of a chauffeur-driven Cadillac, while incurring the splenetic criticism of capitalists and conservatives. And of the Church too, since the CROM, eager to eliminate potential rivals, took a tough stance against Catholic unions (which were strong in devout centre-west cities like Guadalajara) and thus contributed to the mounting anticlericalism of the Calles administration. Some revolutionary leaders were also leery of the CROM's rapid rise to power: the military saw organized labour (correctly) as a counterweight to the army; and state governors resented—and sometimes resisted—CROMista mobilization in their own political backyards.

The CROM benefited from the buoyant economic conditions of 1921–7, when real wages tended to rise and, with them, urban consumption, to the benefit of Mexican manufacturers. As the pie grew larger, the unions could take a bigger slice for their members (and even some non-organized workers benefited), without seriously threatening business confidence and corporate profits. In general, business—including foreign business—did well during these years; denunciations of Calles and Morones's irresponsible radicalism were partly for effect. Certainly, urban business did not face the kind of existential threat which landlords—like the ill-fated Rosalie Evans—confronted. But from 1927 the economy flatlined; the Cristero rebellion took a severe economic toll; and, after 1929, the Depression hit a flaccid economy. It now became harder for the CROM to balance loyalty to the regime with real benefits for its members.

The political crisis which followed the assassination of Obregón also gave Morones's many enemies the chance—as it were—to kill 'the pig of the Revolution', at least politically. The rumour spread that Morones, fancying himself as *presidenciable* (presidential material), was involved in Obregón's death. It was a baseless rumour, but Calles deemed it politic to throw the pig to the wolves; Morones was gaoled and the fortunes of the CROM—always heavily dependent on official patronage—began to tumble. Organized labour, about to face the challenge of the Great Depression, entered a period of flux and realignment that would last until the mid-1930s.

## The excluded middle

In contrast to labour—and, to a lesser degree, the peasantry—the Mexican middle classes were the great unorganized. Seduced by Madero, many had played a part in the genesis of the Revolution; and, even after Maderista democracy failed, middle-class activists were to be found throughout the emerging political and bureaucratic hierarchies of the revolutionary regime. But they enjoyed no collective corporate representation, as workers and peasants did. Outside the regime, many of the middle class felt that, as the Revolution, in its Sonoran incarnation, took over the state and spawned its own 'hegemonic' party, it cynically betrayed its liberal origins (which was true) and turned into a species of corrupt populistic machine politics (which was partly true but very far from the whole truth).

Middle-class criticism of the *revolución-hecha-gobierno*, though predictably articulate, was never very effective. Two main camps were apparent: liberal and Catholic. (And students, overwhelmingly middle-class, were present in both camps. As yet still a small, but emergent, constituency, students tended towards conservatism; the generation of mass radical activism had to await the 1950s and 1960s.) Liberal middle-class critics harked back to Madero and *Antirreeleccionismo*; they called for free elections and campaigned against local caciques and state bosses; but they lacked the *palanca*—the leverage—to achieve results. In 1929, when an emergency presidential election was held, to fill the gap created by Obregón's assassination, the official candidate—Pascual Ortiz Rubio, an admittedly feeble placeman handpicked by *jefe máximo* Calles—faced a robust challenge from José Vasconcelos and his—note the label—Partido Antirreeleccionista.

Vasconcelos was a prominent intellectual, a much-travelled writer and philosopher who had stood alongside Madero in 1910–11 and, a decade later, had briefly served as Minister of Education, patronizing the Mexican muralists and committed to bringing not only literacy but also classical learning—Plato, Dante, Goethe—to Mexico's benighted peasants. A classic intellectual-in-politics, Vasconcelos was strong on rhetoric, weak on delivery. Predictably, his presidential campaign, though it did not lack for widespread and idealistic support, ran up against the steamroller—as he called it—of the PNR and the revolutionary state. His followers were harassed, in a few cases killed; and the lacklustre official candidate won by a street. Politically defunct, Vasconcelos now veered sharply to the Right (by the mid-1930s he had become an admirer of Hitler and Mussolini—a fate which he shared with several disillusioned revolutionary veterans). But the raw material of his anti-reelectionist campaign—the disgruntled urban middle classes—remained politically restless and, in the decades to come, gradually grew in both numbers and influence.

## Church–State conflict: causes

In contrast to Vasconcelos's liberals, middle-class Catholics—those, that is, who premised their politics on their religious affiliation—had the advantage of greater numbers, better organization, and, more importantly, powerful allies, both at home and abroad. This raises the key question of Church–State conflict, which came to dominate Mexican politics in the later 1920s, culminating in the bloody Cristero War (1926–9), which took its name from the war cry of the Catholic rebels: 'Viva Cristo Rey!' ('long live Christ the King!'). The immediate cause of the conflict was the radical anticlerical thrust of the Calles government, which contrasted with the more relaxed attitude of Obregón's administration and, even more starkly, with Madero's benign tolerance of Catholic political activism back in 1911–13. So, what were the causes and consequences of revolutionary anticlericalism?

Conflict between Church and State was not new in Mexican history: it dated back at least to the late colonial period (when the Bourbon Crown sought to clip the wings of an over-mighty Church) and it became more virulent after independence as the nascent liberal party, following Bourbon precedent, stripped the Church of its vast landed wealth, as well as its judicial privileges (*fueros*). These policies, common throughout Latin America at the time, were designed to boost the economy and foster secular national institutions (in respect of justice and family life). They did not challenge Catholicism, still less religion, per se; most liberals were themselves Catholics. Nevertheless, the attack on the Church prompted strenuous, including violent, resistance, which fed into the bitter civil wars of the mid-19th century. Díaz, though a liberal, doused the embers of conflict and established a modus vivendi with the Church; and, with a few exceptions (such as the radical PLM), the early revolutionaries did not see anticlericalism as a high priority. However, given the undoubted strength of Mexico's Catholic Church (a strength now derived less from land or wealth than from its control of hearts and minds, which had increased during the long Pax Porfiriana), the potential for anticlericalism remained and, after 1911, two principal factors turned potential into actual conflict.

First, the Revolution prompted a rapid 'massification' of politics (to call it 'democratization' might be misleading, since pristine democratic procedures were hardly the norm; but it certainly involved an 'empowerment' of sectors of the population who had been politically marginal under Díaz). Since most Mexicans were Catholics, and a good many were political Catholics (that is, they took their political cues from the Church), political Catholicism now became a force in the land, especially in the centre-west of the country—states like Guanajuato, Jalisco, and Michoacán—where the Church was traditionally strong, had grown stronger under Díaz and, in many towns and villages, provided the most influential figure in the politico-cultural milieu: the *cura*, the parish priest.

Under Madero, the Catholic Party flourished, embracing a range of political positions: a minority on the Left, inspired by Pope Leo XIII's bull Rerum Novarum (1891), embraced 'social Catholicism', advocating, albeit in paternalist fashion, rights for workers and peasants; while a majority leaned to the Right, stressing order, hierarchy, and respect for religion (at least, for Catholicism: Protestantism was seen as a dangerous alien import, even a stalking horse for American imperialism). Backed by an influential press, political Catholics made electoral gains and incurred the opposition of liberals who feared a revival of their old clerical enemies. However, prior to 1913, these tensions were chiefly confined to the centre-west and did not assume national prominence.

Second, the military coup of February 1913—a crucial conjunctural factor—impinged upon a society already undergoing a process—perhaps a 'structural' process—of 'massification'. The coup, we have seen, sharpened political enmities: the revolutionaries of 1913 had little of Madero's ingenuous optimism; and, in vowing to crush their enemies, they increasingly included the Church—or, at least, the Catholic leadership—among the ranks of the enemy. For this, though they no doubt exaggerated for the sake of effect, they had real justification: the (powerful) conservative wing of the Church applauded the coup; and sermons were preached and Te Deums sung to welcome Huerta's supposed restoration of order. The PCN bloc in Congress lent the new administration its support and several prominent Catholic *políticos* served in Huerta's cabinet.

The revolutionary response varied: popular leaders like Villa and Zapata tended to be less anticlerical; and, whatever they thought about the Church hierarchy, peasant rebels were usually 'folk-Catholics'—that is, they respected Catholic symbols and rituals, even if, like Zapata, they lived lives unconstrained by the niceties of official Christian morality. The Zapatistas, while fond of hard liquor, cockfighting, and common-law unions, typically wore Virgin of Guadalupe badges in their broad sombreros. The northern revolutionaries—Carranza, Obregón, Calles—took a stronger line against the Church: in part, this reflected their northern origins (the north being traditionally more liberal and anticlerical); but it also derived from their education—liberal, patriotic, steeped in the cult of Benito Juárez—and from their immediate experience of the Revolution when, they alleged, the Church had connived with militarist Reaction and therefore deserved retribution. The Carrancista/Sonoran blueprint for an integrated, nationalist, and progressive Mexico thus required a frontal attack on the Church.

Some radical anticlericals, like Calles, wanted to go even further: they would not only veto Catholic politicization (which the 1917 Constitution did, banning confessional parties or clerical involvement in politics); they would also strike at the root of Catholic power by eliminating the Church's control of hearts and minds. This was a radically ambitious policy, which went far beyond the moderate liberal anticlericalism of the 19th century: the radicals of 1917 sought to abolish all religious education (in the end, a compromise allowed religious secondary, but not primary schooling; however, all schools were to follow a secular curriculum); and they imposed a ban on all public manifestations of religious ritual, which posed a mortal threat to Mexico's rich tradition of public fiestas, processions, and pilgrimages.

In addition to these negative sanctions—which were only partially enforced—the revolutionaries promoted secular public education and enlisted artists and intellectuals in the battle against clerical/Catholic power. Although the armed revolution had interrupted educational provision, the renewed emphasis of the 1920s brought rapid results: by 1928 there were 36 per cent more primary schools than there had been twenty years before, while the number of pupils had risen by 81 per cent; new Federal schools—funded and controlled by the central government—accounted for most of this growth. As growth continued through the 1930s, the Federal government acquired a powerful engine of social acculturation and political mobilization, especially in the countryside. Adult literacy rates steadily rose, from 30 per cent in 1910 to 36 per cent in 1930 and 44 per cent in 1940.

Educational provision was a slow, unspectacular, but broadly successful means to extend the reach of the revolutionary state. More eye-catchingly, the government commissioned huge didactic murals which, gracing the walls of public buildings, were supposed to inculcate revolutionary values-secularism, nationalism and progress-in the hearts and minds of the—largely illiterate—masses. The murals of Diego Rivera thus depicted fat, despotic, and debauched priests who had connived with Spanish conquistadors in the past and who still consorted with oppressive capitalists and bosses in the present. Rivera—seconded by Orozco and Siqueiros—soon went beyond their official brief, including corrupt revolutionary *políticos* in their pictorial polemics; some, including Rivera and Siqueiros, became stalwarts of the infant Mexican

Communist Party, further incurring the wrath of their official patrons (like Vasconcelos). However, radical muralism captured something of the politico-cultural polarization of the time, when the Church was seen, not just as a bastion of wealth and privilege, but also as a source of cultural backwardness, and a major obstacle to the forward march of the Revolution.

The implementation of the anticlerical provisions of the 1917 Constitution was halting: Carranza and Obregón had bigger concerns (above all, survival); and the experience of radical state governors, like General Diéguez of Jalisco in 1918, was that Catholic resistance to anticlerical measures, resistance which in Jalisco included an economic boycott, could prove effective. Obregón, generally pragmatic in his politics, also needed American diplomatic recognition, which, given the vocal Catholic lobby in the US, could be jeopardized by anticlerical policies. Calles, taking office in 1924, was less inhibited. He inherited a stable regime and a buoyant economy; he enjoyed US recognition from the outset; and he was known as a more radical *comecuras*, who saw the assault on the Church as the central plank of his revolutionary platform.

Indeed, Calles and his supporters were—correctly—described as jacobins, in the French revolutionary mould: they advocated a centralized, nationalist, and secular Republic (and were ready to use force to achieve it); they did not repudiate market capitalism (Calles and his cronies often talked of 'socialism': what they meant was a social equilibrium between labour and capital, with the state playing a mediating and managerial role); but they placed great emphasis on politico-cultural social engineering—that is, using state power, including art and education, to foster revolutionary citizenship, which meant undercutting, even eliminating, the influence of their great rival, the Catholic Church.

In pushing this jacobin project, Calles was not alone; regional bosses like Zuno in Jalisco and Garrido Canabál in Tabasco implemented radical anticlerical measures in the provinces. In Tabasco, the state replaced religious fiestas with those dedicated to patriotic anniversaries or to wholesome local products like the pineapple and coconut; prize cattle were paraded carrying labels reading 'the pope' or 'the archbishop'; and officials promoted iconoclastic rituals, at which church icons were chopped up or set ablaze (thus demonstrating their uselessness). Like their French counterparts, Mexico's jacobins thus set out to create a kind of secular, revolutionary, and nationalist 'religion', in order to wean the people away from superstition.

Mainstream Mexican opinion tended to be indifferent or hostile, which is to say that jacobinism was a minority view; it was also a strongly masculine, macho view, which saw women as the weaker vessels through whom the Church exercised its pernicious influence. (It was for this reason that, when President Cárdenas sought to introduce female suffrage in 1937, Congress stalled, fearful that women would vote as the parish priest instructed them; hence women did not get to vote in national elections until 1953, by which time Church–State conflict had subsided). In his visceral opposition to the Church and Catholicism, Calles was unusually dogmatic and assertive—perhaps, it has been suggested, because of the taint of illegitimacy which attached to him. But he was also a powerful and ambitious president, who, as he put it, wanted to be 'master in his own house'.

Calles ratcheted up anticlerical measures, implementing provisions of the 1917 Constitution which had lain fallow. The 1925 Calles Law obliged all priests to register with the state; which meant that the state could effectively control how many priests—and which priests—could officiate. If this was the stick, Calles also provided a sort of carrot, encouraging the creation of a Mexican Schismatic Church, a state-sponsored, 'Erastian' Church which, it was hoped, would draw support away from its Catholic rival. It had very modest success (though recent research shows that its impact was not negligible); however, coupled with other measures, it provoked Catholic protests, both within Mexico and abroad, which culminated in a Church strike (the cessation of all church services beginning in August 1926) and, soon after, a major Catholic rebellion, the so-called Cristiada.

## The Cristero War

The ensuing war lasted three years (1926–9) and tested the revolutionary state's military capacity to the limit. Since the Cristiada was, by definition, an anti-revolutionary movement, committed to the destruction of the new state, it cannot be considered part of the Revolution, so its place in this—very short—history must be brief (it appears, negatively, as a challenge, rather than positively, as a mass movement of aggrieved Catholics). A few points are crucial. First, like the Revolution, the Catholic Church (broadly defined) was a diverse movement/ institution which, for all its centralized and authoritarian structure, pulled in different directions. Rather like the early Revolution of 1910–11, the Cristiada was primarily the work of rural people, the majority of them peasants, who took up arms on the basis of deep grievances; urban Catholics, while they might support the cause, were secondary. Revolutionary critics attributed the Cristiada to top-down manipulation by devious priests, in cahoots with reactionary landlords. While this view—straight out of Rivera's murals—had a basis in truth (some *curas* did preach against land reform and even connived in the elimination of agrarian radicals, like Primo Tapia), nevertheless the Cristiada, like the early Revolution, was a genuine 'bottom-up' popular movement, which did not depend crucially on clerical incitement and organization. In fact, few *curas* were directly involved in the rebellion: most fled to the cities (or abroad), leaving lay Cristeros in control.

Furthermore, the Cristeros' chief grievances concerned less land reform than religion itself, and the threat to religion posed by state anticlericalism. In this sense, they rebelled for the reasons they affirmed, and the nub of the dispute concerned the place of the Church and Catholicism in Mexican 'revolutionary' society. However, that dispute had several dimensions. Land reform—which some priests denounced—and private property rights, which the Church roundly endorsed, were relevant issues. But more important, as recent research shows, was local autonomy: the desire of communities to run their own affairs without external interference. That collective desire had underpinned some of the pioneer ('serrano') rebellions of the Revolution, which sought to shuck off oppressive Porfirian rule. Now, in the 1920s, the external interference came from the centralizing revolutionary state, which strove to curtail or even eliminate the role of the Church in local communities. Popular *curas* might be removed; Catholic education was under threat; public religious rituals—fiestas, pilgrimages, processions—were banned. Such measures struck at the heart of community life, especially in regions where the Church was strong, where ritual flourished, and the *cura* was often the cultural kingpin of the community. Especially under Calles, revolutionary anticlericalism thus posed a direct threat, not just to reactionary landlords and their cronies, but also to the sociocultural life of (some) communities.

This 'autonomist' feature of Cristero resistance helps explain a striking feature of the rebellion: its marked regional pattern, whereby it was very strong in the centre-west, but much weaker, even non-existent, in much of the north, the centre, and the south—even though Callista policy had affected all regions of the country and, indeed, Tabasco under Garrido Canabál represented the acme of revolutionary anticlericalism. The centre-west was strongly Cristero, first, because it was strongly Catholic and clerical: that is, the clergy, in respect of their numbers, institutional footprint, and socio-political influence, were much more powerful here than in other parts of Mexico—which might be Catholic (or 'folk-Catholic', in the manner of the Zapatistas), but which were less clerical, less beholden to the authority of priest and bishop.

Second, the centre-west had played a secondary role in the armed revolution. States like Aguascalientes and Jalisco had never been hotbeds of revolt, like Chihuahua or Morelos. There had been less revolutionary mobilization, less political renovation, less popular empowerment. Whereas in Morelos the Zapatistas had acquired substantial local power, in the centre-west the Revolution was less home-grown and familiar, more a matter of external imposition. The Zapatistas were not notably anticlerical and, indeed, many were Catholics who had scant sympathy for Callista anticlericalism; but the Revolution was 'their' Revolution, which had brought real benefits, including land reform and a share of local political power. Such sentiments help explain the weakness of the Cristero appeal in Morelos and much of central Mexico. But in the centre-west—as in the French centre-west in the 1790s—the Revolution was often seen as alien, intrusive, and oppressive. Religion was the nub of the argument, but religion was a banner around which local people, of diverse social (and ethnic) background could rally, in defence of local interests and in opposition to the aggressive intervention of the revolutionary state.

In several respects, therefore, the Cristiada resembled the popular revolution of the previous decade: it obeyed local popular grievances, was directed against an unpopular state, and could mount a formidable guerrilla challenge to the regular army. And the revolutionary army now acquired some of the faults of the old Federals: campaigning against the Cristeros was a dangerous and brutal business, involving atrocities on both sides, and none of the camaraderie which characterized intra-revolutionary combat; desertions were common and it proved difficult to crush the Cristeros or break their will. The most effective pro-government fighters were agraristas—recipients of land grants—who fought under popular revolutionary leaders, like Saturnino Cedillo: an example not only of how land reform served the interests of the state, but also of how it contributed to the Cristero/Catholic view of land reform as criminal and corrupt.

Rather like the early Revolution, too, the military conflict between Church and State reached a stalemate: the Cristeros dominated swathes of the country in their centre-west homeland, protected by local communities, but their dream of toppling the revolutionary state was an illusion; the regular army, better equipped but poorly motivated, could not be definitively defeated, but neither could it snuff out the rebellion. Meanwhile, the regional economy sharply deteriorated and the mounting costs of the campaign undermined government finances.

## International actors

International actors now came into play. The Vatican was traditionally leery of Church–State conflict and preferred bilateral accords (such as the 1929 Lateran Treaty concluded with Mussolini); it saw that the Cristeros could never overthrow the revolutionary state; and it feared that, with churches closed and services halted, continued conflict would jeopardize the Mexican Church—and, indeed, clerical, including papal, control of that Church.

In the US, the Catholic lobby called for action against Calles's 'Bolshevik' state, citing—and wildly exaggerating—revolutionary atrocities. But Catholic protest, however numerous and noisy, was offset by counter-lobbies which advocated 'hands off Mexico'. (The odd logic of anti-Catholic, pro-Mexico politics made strange allies: pacifists and organized labour found themselves in the same camp as the anti-Catholic Ku Klux Klan). Cristero hopes of decisive American support were confounded; but the revolutionary state, weary of the costly conflict and facing a restive army, was prepared to accept a measure of US mediation, in which the new US ambassador to Mexico—the suave and worldly-wise banker, Dwight Morrow—played a key role. In 1929 a settlement was reached: the bulk of the Cristeros laid down their arms (some were then hunted down and killed); church services resumed; and the clergy, in the main, emerged from hiding or returned from exile and resumed their duties, chastened by the experience and leery of further conflict with the state.

Rome, too, urged Mexican Catholics to avoid further direct confrontation with the state and to promote Catholicism by means of discreet apolitical charity and proselytization (hence, the creation of Acción Católica [Catholic Action] as an umbrella organization designed to channel, and also to moderate, Catholic mobilization). The state stuck to its jacobin stance—thus, the ban on confessional parties remained and, indeed, remains to this day—but the authorities often softpedalled anticlerical measures, whose intensity varied from place to place. Calles's expectation that, with churches closed and services suspended, Catholics would lose their faith (at the rate of 2 per cent a month, he had calculated: Calles liked statistics) was proven wrong. Persecution had neither eroded religion nor broken the Church. Some revolutionaries concluded that this was a battle best avoided; but Calles and many of his cronies stuck to their jacobin beliefs and, after a brief hiatus, resumed their anticlerical offensive in 1931.

As Ambassador Morrow's role makes clear, Mexico's Church–State conflict was an international question. It was one of several pending issues which involved the new regime in acrimonious dispute—and, occasionally, constructive dialogue—with foreign powers and interests. In particular, as World War I shredded Europe's power and prestige, the US emerged as by far the most important country with which Mexico had to deal: they shared a porous 2,000-mile border, across which thousands of Mexicans had migrated during the years of revolution; and, while the aggregate flow of foreign direct investment declined, compared to the boom years of late Porfiriato, American economic interests now eclipsed their European rivals, with new investments in mining, oil, real estate, public utilities, and, increasingly, manufacturing. The US also dominated Mexico's foreign trade, taking three-quarters of Mexico's exports in 1924, while providing three-quarters of imports. American diplomatic recognition was also seen as crucial to the making and breaking of regimes—and rebellions—south of the border.

Some of these were familiar features of the bilateral relationship, now accentuated by the rise of US power and the eclipse of Europe. But the Revolution introduced new elements, such as Church–State conflict. The Revolution was not, as I have stressed, radically anti-foreign or xenophobic. In terms of casualties, Americans in Mexico had suffered relatively little during the years of upheaval (proportionately much less than the Chinese, for example). But they inevitably incurred property losses, as well as facing tax hikes, labour demands, and, as the new regime consolidated after 1915, economic nationalist measures, designed to augment state control of the economy. In part, these initiatives derived from the state's desperate need for revenue, especially from the booming oil industry which, at its peak in 1922, provided one-fifth of government revenue. But they also reflected a broader belief—which had been shared by some late Porfirian policy-makers—that it was time to shift the balance of power and advantage away from foreign companies and towards the Mexican state (or, as the wielders of state power preferred to say, towards the nation and the Mexican people).

The revolutionary state therefore had to balance the need for US recognition against the desire to tax and regulate foreign interests. The result was recurrent skirmishing, further aggravated, during the 1920s, by anticlericalism (which offended American Catholics), land reform (which affected some American landlords), and Mexico's policy towards Nicaragua, where support for Sandino and the Liberals meant opposing the US-backed Conservatives. Obregón, desperate for recognition, had to conciliate the US; Calles, more secure, could be more assertive. His enforcement of the constitutional provision which declared Mexican oil to be the property of the nation incurred American opposition, which his anticlerical and Nicaraguan policies exacerbated. In 1927 tensions peaked and—for the last time—there was talk of US armed intervention.

But Calles relented, patching up a deal with the oil companies; the Cristero War reached a messy conclusion in 1929; and Sandino was finally sacrificed on the altar of US–Mexican détente. Meanwhile, the new US Ambassador, the banker Dwight Morrow, set out to cajole, rather than to coerce, the Mexicans into more moderate policies; and, in Calles, he found a ready interlocutor. After 1929, with the Cristero war concluded, Calles reined in the land reform. US–Mexican tensions diminished. But, as the *jefe máximo* tempered his early radicalism and shifted to the Centre, the Revolution seemed to have relinquished its radical momentum. Then the Great Depression struck.

# Chapter 7
# The Depression, Cardenismo, and after (1930–)

## Recession and recovery

The Depression, hitting an already becalmed Mexican economy, had a severe but short-lived effect. Between 1928 and 1932 GDP fell some 18 per cent; but by 1935 the economy had fully recovered, thanks to buoyant exports (chiefly silver and oil), a resilient subsistence sector (which could absorb surplus labour, including many of the 300,000 Mexicans repatriated from the US), and a robust process of import-substitution industrialization, whereby Mexican industry produced goods previously imported from abroad. Compared to other—large—Latin American countries, such as Argentina and Brazil, Mexico was distinctive by virtue of its revolutionary past, which conferred certain advantages: land reform expanded the subsistence sector and boosted popular purchasing power (as did trade union muscle); Mexico, already bereft of foreign credit, did not face a sudden cut-off of external funds; and the political elite, notably the adroit Finance Minister Alberto Pani, were probably more open to heterodox policies than most of their conventional Latin American—indeed, global—counterparts. After 1932, Pani boosted the money supply and, in shrewd proto-Keynesian fashion, rapidly reflated the economy.

Thus, structural features of the economy, coupled with 'revolutionary' policy, helped achieve a much more rapid recovery than in the US. However, the Depression also had a more profound effect on the trajectory of the Revolution: schematically, we can say that that ('endogenous') trajectory, intersecting with the 'exogenous' impact of the Depression, brought about the last and most radical phase of revolutionary policy, associated with—but not reducible to—the presidency of Lázaro Cárdenas (1934–40). Calles, still the dominant figure in Mexican politics, initially adopted a cautious even conservative approach to the economic downturn: he sought to balance the budget, cut expenditure, and rein in both land reform and the labour movement. (At the same time, he resumed his anticlerical clobbering of the Church, seeking to limit its powers, while promoting secular, even so-called 'socialist' education in the burgeoning federal school system.)

But his economic policy proved predictably inadequate, while the social impact of the Depression stimulated popular militancy. As the CROM dwindled, more radical labour organizations arose, finally, in 1936, crystallizing in the CTM (Confederación de Trabajadores de México: Confederation of Workers of Mexico), which, led by the fiery Marxist orator and intellectual Vicente Lombardo Toledano, proclaimed itself to be 'for a classless society'. As the economy rapidly revived after 1932, strikes proliferated, with workers clawing back what had been lost during the Depression; and, in some sectors, where powerful new national industrial unions emerged (among the railwaymen, miners, electricians, and oil workers), they secured collective contracts which enhanced income, perks, job security, and union muscle. In particular, these contracts embodied 'closed shop' agreements, which gave the *sindicatos* substantial control over hiring and firing, to the disgust of employers, but to the great advantage of union members and, even more, of union officialdom. No other Latin American country boasted an equivalent history of syndical militancy and success during the decade of Depression.

In the countryside, too, unemployment exacerbated the old demand for land, while policy-makers, hitherto sharply divided on the issue, now veered towards radical land reform, which even pragmatic, business-friendly leaders, like interim president Abelardo Rodríguez (1932–4), advocated, on the grounds that it would boost rural income to the benefit of Mexican industry (which proved correct). It also provided a subsistence cushion for the unemployed—including those expelled from the US—who could, as they said in the countryside, 'go back to the *quelite*', that is, eke out a basic existence back on the farm (*quelite* being a kind of wild spinach: nutritious, if unappetizing). Revived worker and peasant militancy thus conspired with a pragmatic radicalization of the revolutionary elite.

## Cárdenas and Cardenismo

In 1933, Calles—still the *jefe máximo* of the regime—tapped the young ex-governor of the state of Michoacán, Lázaro Cárdenas (see Figure 7), as president for the next six-year term. Though a known radical, Cárdenas was also Calles's protégé who, it was

7. President Lázaro Cárdenas (1934–40) meeting with peasants in his home state of Michoacan: adopting an itinerant style of leadership, Cárdenas 'went to the people', especially the peasants, and rapidly accelerated the revolutionary land reform programme.

assumed (not least by Calles himself), would defer to his mentor, as the three previous presidents had done. But, once inaugurated, Cárdenas, who had joined the revolution back in 1913 as an idealistic 17-year-old, broke with the 'big boss', stripping Calles and his cronies of political office, at the same time bolstering the authority of the presidency.

Cárdenas espoused an itinerant populist and paternalistic politics, criss-crossing the country, visiting remote communities, establishing a dialogue with workers and peasants. He spent one-quarter of his six-year term out in the provinces, which earned him the derision of some sophisticated city folk. Workers and peasants, aware of Cárdenas's radical record and sympathies, could now look to the 'Centre' for support; the new-born CTM, as well as the small but growing Communist Party, backed Cárdenas, while agrarian lobbying and land seizures gathered pace. Hacienda communities—that is, communities of resident peons who, hitherto, had been largely debarred from petitioning for land—were now afforded the same rights as independent villagers.

The process of land reform thus greatly accelerated: Cárdenas distributed some 19 million hectares (50 per cent more than all previous presidents put together) and much of this was the fruit of direct presidential initiatives, as the official 'green train' steamed across the country, or the president, reputedly, rode into remote villages on horseback or swam across swollen rivers in order to reach far-flung communities. (Compared to many of his fellow-*políticos*, Cárdenas kept in good shape; he was also considered to be unusually resistant to bribery and corruption.) Apart from extending and accelerating the *reparto*, Cárdenas also pioneered the new collective ejidos, that is, block grants which transformed entire commercial haciendas into peasant (*ejidatario*) cooperatives.

The results of land reform varied, not least according to market trends. The showpiece cotton ejidos of La Laguna succeeded (production was maintained and the *ejidatarios* prospered), but the henequen ejidos of Yucatán—victims of declining demand and a botched reform—were a failure. The more traditional subsistence (corn and beans) ejidos also varied; however, the net result was a modest improvement in peasant livelihood, including rural education, since with ejidos came Federal primary schools, now committed to a radical 'socialist' curriculum. The latter, in addition to secularism, science, and anticlericalism, inculcated class-consciousness, solidarity with workers and peasants, and revolutionary nationalism at home, resistance to fascism and support for the embattled Spanish Republic abroad. Eagerly welcomed by many communities, 'socialist' schools offended conservative Catholic opinion, thus further polarizing opinion.

It is often said that the agrarian reform merely replaced the hegemony of hacienda and landlord with that of the state and its agrarian bureaucracy, which had hardly been the goal of pioneer peasant revolutionaries like Zapata. While partly true, the comparison underestimates the way that these two 'hegemonies' differed. Ejidos were in no sense idyllic rustic utopias (and, postwar, as population grew and state support dwindled, they tended to deteriorate); however, as oral accounts make clear, they conferred a measure of independence, education, and even social citizenship which had been absent in the bad old days of the hacienda. As a perceptive American agronomist noted, 'there is a marked difference in the attitude of the *ejidatario*...[compared to] the peon, or day labourer. The former exhibits a sense of pride, a spirit of independence which is in marked contrast to the servility...of the peon. These *ejidatarios*...are on the road to becoming something new in rural Mexico—citizens.' Land reform, coupled with rural education, thus helped bind the peasantry to the revolutionary state, whose penetration of civil society greatly outstripped anything that the narrowly oligarchic Porfiriato had ever achieved. As a result, the revolutionary state proved much more solid and lasting than its old regime predecessor.

## Critics and constraints

Cárdenas was excoriated by a chorus of critics, who were not confined to the anti-revolutionary Right. Calles, denouncing this dangerous lurch to the Left, was exiled (in the old days he might well have been shot; but under Cárdenas elite politics was growing somewhat more decorous, less red-in-tooth-and-claw). Revolutionaries of more conservative bent tended to agree with Calles, but most kept their heads down, parroting radical slogans even as they discreetly subverted radical reforms (hence, reforms were sometimes compromised by official evasion and foot-dragging—the 'weapons of the strong', as it has been called). The urban middle class, facing rising food prices and recurrent strikes, inveighed against peasant idleness and proletarian irresponsibility. Cárdenas, they alleged, was casting Mexico in the ugly image of the Soviet Union. And political Catholics, while they applauded the fall of their *bête noire* Calles and President Cárdenas's retreat from dogmatic anticlericalism, remained bitterly hostile to Cardenista 'socialism'.

But, for all his radicalism (and his pragmatic alliance with the Communist Party), Cárdenas was no Stalin: he lacked both the power and the paranoia. The official party, the PNR, which, renamed the PRM (Partido de la Revolución Mexicana: The Party of the Mexican Revolution), was rejigged along fashionably corporatist lines in 1938, never dominated society in the way that the Communist Party of the Soviet Union (CPSU) did; and Cárdenas had no intention of creating a command economy. The Mexican Six Year Plan of 1933 rhetorically endorsed economic dirigisme, state intervention, social justice, economic nationalism, and secular education. But state spending, while it rose, remained relatively low (just 6 per cent of GDP in 1940, compared to Brazil's 10 per cent and Argentina's 18 per cent); the private sector, especially manufacturing, benefited from the brisk revival of the economy; and Cárdenas's policy towards workers and peasants, while sympathetic, was also pragmatic and paternalistic. Some strikers could count on state support; but some were warned off.

The Anglo-American oil companies were nationalized, but the big mining interests remained in American hands. Peasants, it was made clear, would receive their ejidos at the hands of the bountiful revolutionary state; their new national confederation, the CNC (Confederación Nacional Campesina: National Peasant Confederation), set up in 1938, was deliberately kept separate from the workers' CTM; and in the same year both CNC and CTM were folded into the new corporate party, thus placed under a form of state tutelage. The benefits, by way of pay, perks, land, and schools, were real; but they came at a cost—accepting the hegemony and, in some measure, the clientelistic control of the state and the burgeoning official party.

In short, Cardenismo represented a genuine reaffirmation of several of the basic tenets—and practices—of the institutional Revolution, in the context of the Depression and the president's conflict with Calles. In addition, while Calles remained a classic jacobin, committed to cultural transformation (changing hearts and minds in order to strengthen the State and weaken the Church), Cárdenas placed greater emphasis on socio-economic transformation (such as land and labour reform). He rowed back on the extremes of anticlericalism, sacking priest-baiters like Garrido Canabal, and maintaining good relations with priests in his home state of Michoacán. While, to the disgust of devout Catholics, the so-called 'socialist' curriculum of the expanding Federal school system stressed secularism, science, and social justice, Cárdenas relaxed anticlerical restrictions, allowing churches to reopen and priests to minister. When the English Catholic novelist Graham Greene visited Mexico in 1938, expecting to find virulent persecution, he was too late; so he had to rely on fantasy and exaggeration to make his preconceived case. Church–State conflict could not be turned off like a tap; there were too many old scars and rancours, while 'socialist' education, even though it was only sketchily implemented, offended strict Catholic opinion. But the trend was towards détente, which would accelerate under Cárdenas's successor, the self-proclaimed 'believer', President Manuel Avila Camacho.

## Labour, oil, and international relations

In the round, the Cardenista reforms were unusually radical by Mexican as well as Latin American standards, at least until the Cuban Revolution of 1959 set a new standard. There can be no doubt that, absent the armed revolution and the political process which it set in motion, they would not have happened. But they were not—despite rhetorical claims to the contrary—a faithful fulfilment of the goals of the pioneer revolutionaries of 1910–15. Organized labour had played a secondary role in the early Revolution, but now enjoyed benefits and leverage out of proportion to its 'revolutionary' contribution. Real wages rose and the major unions acquired some control over hiring and firing (which would form the basis of an enduring syndical clientelism). In 1937 the bankrupt railways were—briefly—handed over to their workers to run. A year later, following a protracted labour dispute, the Anglo-American oil companies were expropriated and turned into a state monopoly, PEMEX.

For some, this radical step was the culmination of a deep Machiavellian plot on the part of Cárdenas and his leftist cronies; in fact, it was a bold improvised response to immediate circumstances, in which a militant union confronted intransigent foreign bosses who insouciantly defied the authority of the Mexican state and impugned the good faith of the president. Fearing the economic effects of a prolonged shutdown, and goaded by the companies' defiance of Mexican sovereignty, Cárdenas took the bold step of expropriating them, thus creating the first major state oil company in the so-called Third World. The expropriation was welcomed by huge public demonstrations (see Figure 8), evidence not only of the popularity of revolutionary

8. Crowds celebrate the March 1938 nationalization of the Anglo-American oil companies by President Cárdenas—the high point of revolutionary economic nationalism.

nationalism, but also of the state's growing capacity to mobilize 'mass publics'—by means of the new institutions which the Revolution had promoted: schools, *sindicatos*, and ejidos. The companies—wrongly—predicted the imminent collapse of the Mexican oil industry. They also sought US government backing, but, given the international climate of 1938–9, the FDR administration was not disposed to risk a quarrel with its southern neighbour at the behest of business interests who were strident opponents of the New Deal.

Indeed, Cárdenas was fortunate that his presidency coincided with that of FDR, while the American ambassador, Josephus Daniels, was both a confidante of Roosevelt and an admirer of Cárdenas, ever keen to draw favourable—if at times fanciful—parallels between Cardenismo and the New Deal. Since war clouds were also gathering over Europe and Asia, the US proved unusually tolerant of Mexican radicalism. Furthermore, Cárdenas's foreign policy was reassuring: he was an outspoken opponent of fascism, denouncing both German and Italian (as well as Soviet) aggression; and he gave aid and comfort to the embattled Spanish Republic, welcoming some 30,000 refugees to Mexico and refusing to recognize the victorious Franco regime. While such policies reassured the US, they further offended conservative and Catholic opinion in Mexico, which sympathized with fascism, especially in its clerical-conservative Falangist form.

International events and ideologies—especially those associated with the Spanish Civil War, which aroused keen interest in Mexico—influenced domestic political alignments. By the later 1930s, several fascist and fascistoid movements had sprung up: those on the secular Right sympathetic to Nazism (and even anti-Semitism); those—more numerous and powerful—on the Catholic Right favouring Franco and the Falange; but all bitterly opposed to Cárdenas and his allegedly pro-Communist policies. Just as the political pendulum had swung to the Left in the early 1930s so, towards the end of the decade, it swung back to the Right. This rightward movement would continue into the 1940s, further impelled by the Second World War and Cold War.

## Retrenchment and retreat

As a result of the oil expropriation, the peso fell, stoking inflation; the 1937 recession in the US had hit Mexico; and, following a spate of social reforms, the Cárdenas administration found itself running a—modest and manageable—budget deficit. Economic and political factors thus combined to boost a diverse and vocal opposition, and the administration, mindful of how political polarization had recently provoked the Spanish Civil War, decided to moderate its course. It made economies, slowed the land reform, and took a tougher line with militant unions (including those in the newly nationalized oil industry).

With hindsight we can see that the tactical retreat of the late 1930s in fact marked a more lasting strategic reorientation of

Mexico's political economy. Cárdenas's chosen successor, President Manuel Avila Camacho (1940–6), was a centrist, hostile to the radical Left and respectful of the Catholic Church; he favoured political conciliation at home and close collaboration with the US abroad. Elected in a bruising and contentious poll in the summer of 1940 (evidence that the official party had by no means mastered the art of discreet electoral fixing), Avila Camacho softpedalled land reform, wound up 'socialist' education, and spurned CTM radicalism. Lombardo Toledano's star faded and the leadership of the CTM passed to Fidel Velázquez, a consummate union boss, who would be a loyal and hard-headed ally of the regime for decades to come.

Avila Camacho's successor, Miguel Alemán (1946–52), the first civilian president of the postrevolutionary period, went much further, purging—and thus deradicalizing—the unions and reorganizing the official party which, in 1946, became the PRI (Partido Revolucionario Institucional: Revolutionary Institutional Party). Central (presidential) control was enhanced, and the PRI—far more 'institutional' than it was 'revolutionary'—became an engine of clientelist politics, enjoying a near-monopoly of office and relying on the old levers of labour and land reform to keep its mass clienteles in line. The institutional apparatus set up in the 1920s and 1930s thus remained, but it increasingly adopted conservative, business-friendly, regressive policies.

## Postscript: the regime of the PRI

The result was a highly durable and successful populist regime, largely civilian and technocratic in make-up, discreetly allied with Mexican business, and, in the chill climate of the Cold War, pragmatically aligned with the US. The old revolutionary generation now faded into history and, with them, the *revolución-hecha-gobierno*. Cárdenas, among the youngest—and healthiest—of revolutionary veterans, survived until 1970, acting as the discreet conscience of the Left within the PRI. But the Left in no sense called the tune. Within the broad church of the ruling party, business-friendly policies (low taxation and high tariffs) prevailed, and, while the Mexican economy grew robustly through the 1950s and 1960s, generating new industrial jobs and drawing rural migrants to the swelling cities, it did so on the basis of growing inequality: a somewhat paradoxical outcome for a regime which still claimed revolutionary provenance and inspiration. Cárdenas openly expressed his radical views on international issues (the Cuban Revolution, the Vietnam War), while—in the main—avoiding overt criticism of the domestic regime of the PRI. That regime, meanwhile, acquired a reputation for political stability and economic success unequalled in Latin America in the postwar generation. Growth was brisk, inflation remained low, and the military deferred to their civilian masters—who were prepared to crush outspoken opponents by force, as the students of 1968 discovered, but who preferred to rely on more subtle forms of clientelistic social control.

The 'revolutionary' dimension of PRI rule thus became increasingly rhetorical: it existed in the name, in the regime's high-flown but often hypocritical rhetoric, in school textbooks and official anniversaries, and in the continually recycled myths and symbols of the Revolution: Madero and democracy; Zapata and land reform; Cárdenas, oil, and economic nationalism. Over time, however, even these revolutionary icons were claimed by opposition movements: on the Right, the loosely Christian-democratic PAN (Partido Acción Nacional: National Action Party), set up in 1939 to challenge Cardenismo, which claimed the democratic mantle of Madero and included several members of the Madero family in its ranks; on the Left, popular and peasant movements which drew on the name and tradition of Zapata, including the 'neo-Zapatista' rebels who rebelled in the southern state of Chiapas in 1994. Insurgent unions, weary of CTM bossism, also harked back to the Revolution while, when the PRI itself suffered a schism in 1987–8, the leftist dissidents who broke away to form the PRD (Partido de la Revolución Democrática), were led by Cárdenas's son, Cuauhtémoc. And when radical students protested in 1968, they carried images of Zapata alongside those of Che Guevara.

The ideas and images of the Revolution thus lived on, but were increasingly detached from the regime to which the Revolution had given birth. Or they were consigned to a folkloric memory bank, where—a tribute to the mythmaking effect of Rivera's murals—Zapata rode his white horse (in fact, Zapata's horse was a sorrel) and the Revolution was recycled to the foot-tapping tunes of old *corridos* (popular ballads) like 'La Cucaracha' ('the cockroach'). Hollywood, too, mined this seam, with a string of mediocre and worse Mexican-revolutionary films, Elia Kazan's *Viva Zapata!* (1952) being a rare exception.

The secret of the PRI's success over many decades, however, was less repetitive discourse and shallow symbolism than the maintenance of a well-oiled political machine—more akin to the Taiwanese Guomingdang than to the CPSU—and its relatively successful, but conservative, stewardship of a fast-growing, low-inflation, job-generating economy. When, in the 1980s, the growth stopped, inflation took off, and jobs dried up, the fortunes of the PRI slumped; and the party leadership opted for a bold neo-liberal turn, which involved finally and formally ditching many of the old shibboleths of the Revolution: the ejido, economic nationalism, and residual anticlericalism. Thus, overt discursive repudiation of revolutionary principles finally caught up with discreet practical abandonment. When the centenary of the Revolution was officially marked in 2010, Mexico's government was in the hands of the PAN, a broadly pro-business, neo-liberal, Catholic-leaning party which had been born, back in 1939, as a direct challenge to and repudiation of the Revolution. The official commemoration was anodyne, even inept. But in some parts of the country, and among some social groups, the Revolution—its heroes, exploits, and accomplishments—was more fondly remembered, proof that, if it had long parted company with Mexico's rulers, the Revolution still retained an important place in Mexico's collective memory.

# Further reading

The best general guide to modern Mexican history, including the
Revolution, is the multi-authored *Mexico Since Independence*
(Cambridge, 1991), edited by Leslie Bethell. Readers of Spanish can
also choose from the twenty-three-volume series, *Historia de la
revolución mexicana*, edited by Luis González and published by the
Colegio de México between 1978 and 1983: well researched and amply
illustrated, it advances methodically through 1911–60. Paul Garner,
*Porfirio Díaz* (London, 2001) provides a short, accessible, somewhat
charitable, portrait of the prerevolutionary president. Alan Knight,
*The Mexican Revolution* (2 vols, Cambridge, 1986), is a detailed study
of the armed revolution (1910–20), its causes, course, and character.
John Mason Hart, *Revolutionary Mexico: The Coming and Process of
the Mexican Revolution* (Berkeley, 1987), adopts a fairly traditional
Marxist approach; Michael Gonzales, *The Mexican Revolution,
1910–40* (Albuquerque, NM, 2002), is a more middle-of-the-road
overview. Enrique Krauze, *Mexico: Biography of Power. A History
of Modern Mexico, 1810–1996* (New York, 1997), is a top-down,
political-biographical narrative, broadly critical of the Revolution and
its outcome. Anita Brenner, *The Wind that Swept Mexico: The History
of the Mexican Revolution of 1910–42* (New York, 1943, since
reprinted) offers good visual images.

Two big biographies of the pre-eminent popular leaders of the
Revolution are classics: John Womack Jr, *Zapata and the Mexican
Revolution* (New York, 1969), an evocative and sympathetic study of
Zapatismo; and Friedrich Katz's *The Life and Times of Pancho Villa*
(Stanford, CA, 1998), which combines balance and detail. Samuel

Brunk, *Emiliano Zapata! Revolution and Betrayal in Mexico* (Albuquerque, NM, 1995) is also valuable, as well as being rather more critical of its subject. The radical American journalist John Reed penned a graphic—at times imaginative—account of the northern Revolution, particularly Villismo: *Insurgent Mexico* (New York, 1914).

Rodney D. Anderson, *Outcasts in their Own Land: Mexican Industrial Workers, 1906–11* (DeKalb, IL, 1976) remains the best study of prerevolutionary organized labour; Ramon Eduardo Ruiz, *Labor and the Ambivalent Revolutionaries: Mexico, 1911–23* (Baltimore, 1976) continues the story through years of revolution.

Local and regional studies have been crucial in deepening our understanding of the Revolution: D. A. Brading, ed., *Caudillo and Peasant in the Mexican Revolution* (Cambridge, 1980), was a pioneering symposium; Thomas Benjamin and Mark Wasserman, eds, *Provinces of the Revolution: Essays on Mexican Regional History, 1910–29* (Albuquerque, NM, 1990), is also useful, if variable. Luis González y González, *San José de Gracia: Mexican Village in Transition* (Austin, TX, 1982), a translation of a (1968) classic, traces the history of a single—conservative, Catholic—community in western Mexico from its 19th-century foundation through the Porfiriato, Revolution, Cristero War, and Cardenismo.

The foreign relations of the armed revolution are studied in great detail by Friedrich Katz, *The Secret War in Mexico: Europe, The United States and the Mexican Revolution* (Chicago, 1981); Mark T. Gilderhus, *Diplomacy and Revolution: US-Mexican Relations under Wilson and Carranza* (Tucson, AZ, 1977) offers a sensible account of a contentious topic. Jonathan C. Brown, *Oil and Revolution in Mexico* (Berkeley, 1993) convincingly dispels some of the polemical hype that has surrounded the oil industry; Lorenzo Meyer, *Mexico and the United States in the Oil Controversy, 1917–42* (Austin, TX, 1977) also remains useful.

The lives of the two Sonoran leaders who rose to dominate Mexican politics in the 1920s are recounted in Linda Hall, *Alvaro Obregón: Power and Revolution in Mexico, 1911–20* (College Station, TX, 1981) and Jürgen Buchenau, *Plutarco Elías Calles and the Mexican Revolution* (Lanham, MD, 2007). On the crucial Church–State conflict of the 1920s, Jean Meyer, *The Cristero Rebellion: The Mexican*

*People between Church and State, 1926–29* (Cambridge, 1976), is a very abbreviated translation of the author's monumental revisionist study, *La Cristiada* (Mexico, 1977–9). Innovative recent research on the same subject is represented in Matthew Butler, ed., *Faith and Impiety in Revolutionary Mexico* (New York, 2007). Ernest Gruening, *Mexico and its Heritage* (New York, 1928) is a classic eye-witness account of 1920s Mexico, written by a perceptive and well-informed American journalist. Robert Freeman Smith, *The United States and Revolutionary Nationalism in Mexico, 1916–34* (Chicago, 1972), provides a sophisticated study of US–Mexican relations.

Jeff Bortz, *Revolution within the Revolution: Cotton Textile Workers and the Mexican Labor Regime, 1910–23* (Stanford, CA, 2008), stresses shopfloor radicalism; while Joe C. Ashby, *Organized Labor and the Mexican Revolution Under Lázaro Cárdenas* (Chapel Hill, NC, 1967) remains a solid study of 1930s labour.

There is no convincing overview of the key process of agrarian mobilization and land reform, though Eyler N. Simpson, *The Ejido: Mexico's Way Out* (Chapel Hill, NC, 1937) remains a classic—and compendious—eye-witness analysis; and, apart from the biographical and regional studies cited above, contrasting case-studies are provided by Paul Friedrich, *Agrarian Revolt in a Mexican Village* (Englewood Cliffs, NJ, 1970), a succinct anthrohistorical account of Primo Tapia's struggle in Naranja, Michoacán; and Timothy J. Henderson, *The Worm in the Wheat: Rosalie Evans and Agrarian Struggle in the Puebla-Tlaxcala Valley of Mexico, 1906–27* (Durham, NC, 1998), a graphic account of Mrs Evans's failed crusade against popular agrarianism.

Regional diversity is, again, displayed in Ben Fallaw, *Religion and State Formation in Postrevolutionary Mexico* (Durham, NC, 2013), which complements Mary Kay Vaughan, *Cultural Politics in Revolution: Teachers, Peasants and Schools in Mexico, 1930–40* (Tucson, AZ, 1997), a perceptive analysis of state–society relations in the 1930s. By contrast, Graham Greene, *The Lawless Roads* (London, 1939), is a dyspeptic tirade, which tells us more about its author than about Mexico.

The broad political economy of the 1930s is convincingly treated by Nora Hamilton, *The Limits of State Autonomy: Postrevolutionary*

*Mexico* (Princeton, 1982), while James W. Wilkie, *The Mexican Revolution: Federal Expenditure and Social Change* (Berkeley, 1967), usefully calibrates the scale and character of state spending through the 20th century.

Thomas Benjamin, *Revolución: Mexico's Great Revolution as Memory, Myth and History* (Austin, TX, 2000), carefully charts the formation of the 'official myth' of the Revolution, whose rise and fall is also addressed by Alan Knight, 'The Myth of the Mexican Revolution', *Past and Present*, 209 (2010), 223–73.

Comparative studies of great revolutions tend to slight Mexico: a fine exception is Eric R. Wolf, *Peasant Wars of the Twentieth Century* (New York, 1969), whose chapter on Mexico remains cogent; Samuel P. Huntington, *Political Order in Changing Societies* (New Haven, 1968), chap. 5, shoehorns Mexico into a strange east/west typology; while Alan Knight, 'Revisionism and Revolution: Mexico Compared to England and France', *Past and Present*, 134 (1992), 159–99, draws parallels between the recent historiography of the English, French, and Mexican Revolutions.

# Index

## Q

## R

## S

## T

Index

# Expand your collection of
# VERY SHORT INTRODUCTIONS

# SOCIAL MEDIA
## Very Short Introduction

## Join our community
www.oup.com/vsi

- Join us online at the official Very Short Introductions **Facebook** page.
- Access the thoughts and musings of our authors with our online **blog**.
- Sign up for our monthly **e-newsletter** to receive information on all new titles publishing that month.
- Browse the full range of Very Short Introductions online.
- Read **extracts** from the Introductions for free.
- Visit our library of **Reading Guides**. These guides, written by our expert authors will help you to question again, why you think what you think.
- If you are a teacher or lecturer you can order inspection copies quickly and simply via our website.

# ONLINE CATALOGUE
## A Very Short Introduction

Our online catalogue is designed to make it easy to find your ideal Very Short Introduction. View the entire collection by subject area, watch author videos, read sample chapters, and download reading guides.

http://fds.oup.com/www.oup.co.uk/general/vsi/index.html